... IN BED WITH
BROADCASTING

A Memoir

KEN DAVIS

Cover Design – Doug Walker
Design Consultant – Philip Davis
Author Photo – Gary Brainard

Published by Philosopher Press
PRINT ISBN: 978-1-5463-1855-2

DISCLAIMER: Everything herein is my opinion regarding the people and events in my life. While every attempt has been made to verify the information in this book, neither the author nor the publisher assumes any responsibility for errors, omissions, or contrary interpretations of the subject matter.

To Carole, Chris, and Philip

*Because of you, the chapters
of my life keep getting better*

WHAT PEOPLE ARE SAYING ABOUT *IN BED WITH BROADCASTING*...

"From the Hillside Strangler to Phil Spector to Barack Obama, Ken Davis has seen it all and covered most of it: a thrill ride through journalism and our cultural history."
—**Josh Mankiewicz**, network news correspondent

"WOW...! Spellbinding. I felt I was along with Ken every step of the way. I just want to know who is going to portray him in the film!"
—**Joel Tator**, producer/director, NBC, KTLA, KCBS

"I've known Ken Davis as one of the great news editors and producers in the broadcasting business. Ken has more stories than ANYONE I know. He has stories we can laugh at, recoil at, and be inspired by. When you read this, you will hear stories of people you know and don't...but all of them are memorable and insightful. Ken Davis...thanks for your memories!"
—**Roy Firestone**, ESPN

"Ken's story of perseverance and exuberance amid a wildly untamable broadcasting career is inspiring to anyone crazy enough to step aboard."
—**Hettie Lynne Hurtes**, anchorwoman, KPCC (NPR)

"Ken Davis and I have shared desks in some of the most exciting newsrooms in the country. This is a rare chance to really look behind the veil and see what truly goes on behind the scenes from someone who was actually there to see it all."
—**Sam Rubin**, entertainment journalist, KTLA

"When I was a rookie sportscaster in L.A. more than three decades ago, I knew Ken Davis was the real deal because, while all the newspaper guys hated TV, they still used to ask me to send him their regards. He was a pro's pro then and, as *In Bed with Broadcasting* will show you, he remains so today. Plus, how many newsmen met Mae West after she died?"
—**Keith Olbermann**, political and sports commentator

"The splendid little secret of journalism is how damn much fun it is to be right there in the middle of what's happening. Mayhem, Mae West, and murderers, the chimps and the chumps—Ken Davis spills the beans on his fascinating life in broadcasting, all the way from cocktails with Cronkite down to the Kool-Aid punchbowl that is infotainment."
—**Patt Morrison**, columnist and broadcaster

"Ken Davis is the finest TV producer I've ever worked with and I've worked with the best. This is a must read for anyone interested in the broadcasting business!"
—**Billy Griffin**, singer/songwriter; star on the
Hollywood Walk of Fame

"Not only is Ken insightful about the TV industry, but he is also one of the kindest and most caring people in a business that usually fosters neither. I think you will understand that as you relive some behind-the-scenes moments of Ken's mistress ... and mine, too. He does an incredible job of blending together how news and entertainment fueled our lives from the 1970s until today."
—**John Daly,** host of *Real TV* and *Undercover Jetsetter*

"Anyone who works in television or watches it will appreciate Ken's breezy writing style. You can't wait to find out what happens next. If you are a history buff, you will relive many memories when television news was vital, accurate, important, and REAL. As Ken says in this book, television was his mistress and was certainly mine, too!
—**Jeff Wald,** former news director, KTLA, KCOP

"Rivetingly written, filled with amazing anecdotes, and as good and compelling as anything I've read about the business."
—**Steve Weakley,** producer/writer, KNBC, KTLA

"Ken writes almost exactly the way he talks, always a big challenge for writers. I could see myself standing there as the events of his career unfolded. He breathes new life into the real life "characters" we thought we knew, and it's an eye-opener to see how journalism is supposed to work.
— **Bob McCormick**, business news anchorman

"Having spent much of my career on the same roller coaster ride that Ken has been on, I can say his perspective is sharp, accurate, and injects the necessary humor to survive the wild ride of television news."
— **Dana Adams**, former correspondent, NBC, *EXTRA*

"Ken captures an era of reckless abandon that might border on fantastical, if I didn't know and trust the man to his core. His latest chronicle will be the topic of conversation at the Chambers dinner table for years."
— **Jamie Chambers**, reporter, Fox 5 San Diego;
grandson, legendary reporter Stan Chambers

"From serial killers to towering infernos to a dying Oscar winner's final interview, Ken Davis never met a story he couldn't uncover. As a former cubicle-mate in the TV trenches with him, I understand his love-hate relationship. Davis's adventures in newsgathering should be required reading for wanna-be journalists, adrenaline junkies, and truth-seekers alike."
— **Stacey Gualandi**, former reporter/producer, *Inside Edition, EXTRA*

CONTENTS

INTRODUCTION

HAVING SPENT FOUR DECADES working in broadcasting, I've come to understand what the industry is to me: she is my mistress. Together, we hobnobbed with Hollywood royalty, socialized with presidents, and journeyed inside the minds of some of the world's most interesting people. Thanks to her, I won Emmy Awards, earned the confidence of the most trusted man in America, and even helped save a life or two.

But this volatile seductress also pointed a loaded gun to my head, brought me face-to-face with a notorious serial killer, and demanded I sell my soul. She looked hot, but she could be cold and calculating. So, why did I stick around? Well, frankly, she was irresistible. As fickle as she was at times, she was also generous. My mistress opened doors into a world I never could have imagined.

My career transitioned through the same phases as many untamed affairs: *Seduction, Love, Disenchantment, Rebound,* and *Farewell.* Along the way, my mistress and I went through tremendous change, and I learned many lessons I wish I'd known before I succumbed to her siren song. Lessons like: every one of us has a hidden story, self-esteem must come from within, and a sense of humor can be your best friend.

As you're about to find out, I also learned the hard way that it's generally not a wise idea to follow a homicidal maniac down a dark secluded street or to piss-off the heavyweight boxing champion of the world.

Variety has been the spice of my career, and so it is here. Some chapters read like a traditional memoir, while adventures with people like Barack Obama, Walter Cronkite, Phil Spector, Henry Fonda, Bill Cosby, Mae West, and the Hillside Strangler unfold like a Hollywood movie — the scenes so vivid, you'll feel like you're right there with me.

Only a few names have been changed to protect the innocent or, in some cases, spare embarrassment. Except for my own embarrassment. That I generously offer for your unbridled entertainment.

So, kick off your shoes, get ready for a wild ride, and hop *In Bed with Broadcasting*.

SEDUCTION

Seduction is always more singular and sublime than sex and it commands the higher price.

—Jean Baudrillard

CHAPTER 1
LIGHT MY FIRE

Spring 1972

PRESIDENT NIXON *tries to convince us that the Watergate break-in is "just a third-rate burglary"; Don McLean grabs a big slice of record sales with "American Pie"; and, at the tender age of twenty, I become the youngest TV anchorman in the country.*

# # #

"Good evening. Topping tonight's news, a warehouse fire south of Flagstaff continues to burn out of control... What the...? Ow...! Get this thing off me! Uh, we'll be right back after this commercial break."

Thus was the inglorious start to one of my first newscasts at KOAI-TV in Flagstaff, Arizona. A talk show aired in the same studio just before the news, and, since it was "Adopt-a-Pet Day," four-legged critters were everywhere. Mere moments after the floor director counted down "3...2...1" and pointed at me, mouthing "*Go*," a berserk bulldog raced under my desk and promptly turned my ankle into a chew toy.

A moment like this wasn't quite what I'd envisioned when I first met my seductive mistress a decade earlier. Then again, I was just a kid. What the heck did I know?

She first beckoned me from underneath my pillow on Poppyfields Drive in Altadena, California. To my parents, I was asleep, but each night I lay awake for an hour or more, listening to her. I wasn't even a teenager yet, but I quickly fell head over heels. It was the dawn of a torrid affair that would last for decades.

She snuck into my bedroom via a transistor radio tuned to my local rock station—KRLA. Every night, I'd go to bed with what I thought were the greatest sounds this planet had ever produced: The Beach Boys, The Rolling Stones, The Supremes, Bob Dylan. Whether the songs were about love, dancing, or politics, they spoke to my malleable young mind in a language my parents and teachers never could.

Sensing the adults in my life didn't quite get me, I gravitated toward those who I thought did. I took notice of a different set of grown-ups, all happily engaged in rocking the boat. It was those guys with the big voices and crazy antics—the disc jockeys—who enticed me to enter the world of broadcasting. They seemed to be having a great time *all* the time. Secretly, I wanted to be like those DJs. While my family slept, I stood in front of a mirror in striped pajamas, talking into a hairbrush like it was a microphone, doing my darndest to lower my pre-adolescent voice. I'm quite certain our family dog questioned my sanity. No matter. I was hooked.

From there forward, I was bound and determined to figure out how to get into broadcasting. I don't think it was a need for attention, since I've always been blessed to have many friends. In fact, those closest to me will confirm that, hidden behind my outgoing exterior, there lies a shy side.

My best guess is I figured we only have one shot at this thing called life, so why not push the boundaries and go for the gusto?

Beginning about age thirteen, nearly every weekend I hopped on my electric-blue Schwinn bike with its foot-and-a-half-long banana seat and journeyed six miles to KRLA radio in Pasadena, California to watch the disc jockeys ply their magic. DJs like Casey Kasem and Bob Eubanks took a liking to me and made me feel important by letting me answer phones and sort mail. It felt like these guys had entrusted me with the front door key to the Land of Oz.

KRLA became the center of my universe. Music ran through the veins of everyone in the building—their passion became my passion. Bob Eubanks even announced he was mortgaging his house to bring some up-and-coming group called The Beatles to the Hollywood Bowl.

Several years later, I headed off to college in Flagstaff, Arizona. No doubt my college-professor father and former-valedictorian mother would have preferred I major in education, like everyone else in my family, but they had the good sense to let me be me. I majored in political science and minored in staying out of Vietnam.

But my obsession with broadcasting took precedence over all else. Within six months, I got a job playing the hits of the '70s on the local rock radio station: *Coconino County cutup California Ken crankin' out the cream of the crop on KEOS!*

With the energy only a nineteen-year-old could muster, I took a second radio DJ gig on weekends, 140 miles to the south at KUPD in Phoenix.

My radio DJ days in Flagstaff

Somehow, I also managed to carry a full load of college classes. No doubt this was the genesis of my lifelong addiction to caffeine.

Before long, the Watergate political scandal rocked the nation and infected me with the journalism bug. When I wasn't spinning records, trying to get laid, or, on rare occasions, studying, I sat in front of my nineteen-inch Zenith TV, fixated by the non-stop news coverage of the conspiracy.

What should have been a minor news story about a break-in at the headquarters of the Democratic Party ballooned into a constitutional crisis that brought down the president of the United States. I soaked in the suspense of the story and the seriousness of the journalists reporting it. Right then, I knew I wanted to be in the same profession as the broadcasters who were in the thick of the action.

Anchoring the news in Flagstaff

Not long afterward, I dusted off my only suit and knocked on the door of KOAI-TV in Flagstaff. I must have said something right, because they hired me to anchor the news before I was even old enough to buy a beer. I had no business reporting world events at that young stage of life, but I guess they figured I came cheap and looked presentable with a tie.

Our audience for KOAI-TV consisted of Flagstaff-area residents and the sparsely populated Navajo Indian Reservation. We were the number-one TV station in town. Then again, we were the *only* TV station in town.

After graduation, I got a gig as a TV reporter in San Luis Obispo, California. Not only did I love my job, but I lived only a block from the ocean—life was good.

And yet, not even a year into the job, I found myself wanting more. I didn't want to kick back and take it easy. I guess I wanted to be somebody. So I set my sights on the big time: Los Angeles. When a newswriting job opened up at KCOP Television in Hollywood, I packed up my Pinto and headed south.

Anchoring the news in San Luis Obispo

Soon, I was producing the *Ten O'clock News*. We had one of the lowest-rated broadcasts in town, but L.A. was the second-largest market in the country. That meant, every night, I had the privilege of deciding what news stories hundreds of thousands of people would see. News Director Dan Tompkins even had enough faith in me to let me co-anchor the broadcast when the regularly scheduled guy went on vacation.

Working in the entertainment capital of the world fed a hunger in me I didn't know existed. I quickly got caught up in the power, the celebrity, and the magic that is tinsel town. Never did I imagine that this broadcasting industry—this seducer of innocents—would become my complicated mistress who would toy with me for decades to come.

She took form in the people I dealt with every day, but I got my first real taste of her brazen instability when she held me at gunpoint in a twenty-two-room mansion high above the Sunset Strip.

CHAPTER 2

THE NIGHT I LOST THAT LOVIN' FEELING

January 1977 – Hollywood, California

"SOUNDS GREAT, Phil. We'll head up to your place right after we wrap the show." Anchorman Bill Deiz hung up the phone across the desk from me in the KCOP-Television newsroom. I produced the nightly news, and Bill anchored with Hettie Lynne Hurtes.

"Who was that, Bill?" I asked.

"Oh, just some record producer I interviewed years ago. Phil Spector. Says we're his favorite newscast. Wants Hettie and me to come to his house for drinks tonight after the show."

Harvey Phillip Spector a.k.a. Phil Spector, music mogul. Best known as the reclusive genius who wrote and produced dozens of Top 40 hits with his pioneering "Wall of Sound." Saying he was just *some* music producer was like saying Muhammad Ali is just *some* boxer or Meryl Streep is just *some* actress. Brian Wilson of the Beach Boys called him "the biggest musical inspiration of my life." A young Bruce Springsteen talked his way into Spector's recording sessions to emulate his style. When The Beatles needed someone to produce their final album, *Let it Be*, they called on Spector. As for me, the man produced the soundtrack of my youth.

I learned to dance with my neighbor, Elaine Rohde, while listening to "Be My Baby" by The Ronettes.

I had my first schoolboy crush when The Righteous Brothers topped the charts with "You've Lost That Lovin' Feeling."

And I lost my virginity when "Imagine" by John Lennon became the anthem of a generation.

So, when the chance came to meet the world-class recluse in person, I reacted like someone had offered me front-row seats to the Super Bowl.

"Look me right in the eyes, Bill," I said. "If you ever hope to have the lead story again, you're taking me with you."

I couldn't believe Spector singled out the newscast I produced as his personal favorite. In hindsight, this should've been my first clue the guy had a few screws loose.

Sure, back in the day, KCOP launched the careers of everyone from Betty White to Liberace. But by the time I got there, its newscast had the smallest budget this side of Phoenix, not to mention a fledgling producer at the helm— *me*. But somehow, the knowledge that Spector liked the show validated my work.

When the news broadcast ended, Hettie and I piled into Bill's car to head over to Spector's place. In the semi-rush, Bill gave us a warning: "I oughta let you guys know, Phil's a strange dude."

"How so?" Hettie asked.

"Well, to start with, he has a fascination with weapons. I also hear he's got a crazy side."

Fascination with weapons? Crazy side? Gee, what could

possibly go wrong?

We journeyed down Sunset Strip toward the posh Westside. Soon, we passed homes large enough to have their own indoor basketball court. Then, amidst towering pines, there stood Phil Spector's Italianate villa, with its Beverly Hills address and purebred pedigree. The mansion previously belonged to the filthy-rich Woolworth family and later became the setting of Vince's house on the TV show *Entourage.*

We pulled up to the front gate, where a thick protective wall surrounded the property. Lofty trees shrouded the courtyard, while security lights indicated we were under surveillance. Bathed by the light of a full moon, the twenties-era estate seemed to whisper, *"Come inside, my dear, and experience a way of living you've only imagined..."*

A monotone voice caught us by surprise, blaring through a speaker hidden in the bushes. "May I help you?"

Once cleared for admission, we drove up a short driveway into the circular courtyard. Granite statues stood as silent sentries. We parked next to an ominous sign warning us, if we made one wrong move, guard dogs would love to have us for dinner.

Hettie hesitated as she got out of the car. The normally unflappable anchorwoman fidgeted with her hair and stammered, "I think I've seen enough. What do you say we call it a night?"

Bill and I pretended we didn't hear her. A spooky stillness hung in the cool night air as we walked across the wide cement driveway, past a tiered fountain, and cautiously approached the ten-foot-high wooden door. An owl hooted from somewhere in the dark, as if to warn us we were being watched.

One of us rang the bell. I felt like a child encountering

his first haunted house: sixty percent excited, forty percent ready to run like hell.

Moments later, the door slowly creaked open. There stood a tall, muscular fellow with the bone-chilling glare of a professional hit man.

"Good evening. I'm George. I presume you're the TV people?"

After he confirmed our identities, George led us into what can only be described as something out of a movie. Norma Desmond's eerie mansion in the classic old film *Sunset Boulevard* came to mind—a massive monument to memories and old money. The entryway, speckled with dark, antique furniture, was barely visible in the gloomy light. I theorized Spector paid his mortgage with what he saved on electricity bills.

George led us down a candlelit hallway in absolute silence. Portraits of everyone from Lincoln to Lawrence of Arabia seemed to eye our every move, like the paintings in Disneyland's Haunted House. But this was merely an appetizer to our next stop: the living room.

"Unreal," Hettie said, as we hovered at the entry to a room that felt as big as my backyard in Altadena. Your average head of state would have felt right at home underneath the twenty-foot ceiling.

An inviting fire crackled in the colossal fireplace, while the scent of vanilla candles filled the air. A Steinway concert grand piano, begging to be touched by experienced hands, stood next to an ivory chess set that probably cost more than my car. A colorful vintage jukebox played mellow oldies, while, in a far corner, an imposing grandfather clock watched over us.

"Now, aren't you guys glad you joined me?" Bill said.

Hettie could only manage a smile. I nodded a definite

yes.

George invited us to sit on either the rose-colored velvet armchairs or the beige-satin sofa. "I'll tell Mr. Spector you've arrived."

When George turned to fetch his master, I spotted a pistol tucked in his waistband. My blood pressure surged.

Maybe he really is a professional hit man.

The sound of the relentless heartbeat of the grandfather clock reminded us time was passing. Ten, fifteen, twenty minutes went by. While waiting, I remembered what my father once told me: "Nothing good ever happens after midnight."

Finally, a lone figure appeared at the top of the winding staircase. If this were a Spector song, the pounding drums, guitars, and piano would have come to a sudden stop. Making the classic Hollywood entrance, his hand trailing on the bannister, the star of the show strolled down his magnificent staircase, paused for effect, and then broke the silence with his high, nasal voice.

"George, cognac for everyone."

Phil wore designer sunglasses and a black satin bathrobe over matching pajamas. I couldn't help but notice the elevated heels on his shoes, worn to augment his diminutive stature. He spoke with a New York cadence as he surveyed his visitors.

"Bill, it's marvelous to see you again. I'm so glad Hettie joined you. Now, who's this young lad?"

"He's our producer," Bill replied.

"Well, he must be a damned good one. Your newscast is the only one I watch. You guys are much better than a lot of those clowns who call themselves journalists."

I wasn't sure I believed the guy, but, in our business, flattery gets you everywhere. I also sensed Phil had the hots for Hettie.

"Your delivery is a thousand times better than Barbara Walters'," Phil said to our anchorwoman. She beamed.

Within minutes of Phil joining us in the living room, we got along like lifelong buddies. Any sense of intimidation was quickly overcome by two powerful forces: youthful self-confidence and that great equalizer—alcohol.

"Hey, Bill, how about some Manischewitz to wash down that Courvoisier?" I figured Phil must be the only human on the planet who switched back and forth between cheap kosher wine and rare French cognac.

"Uh, sure, Phil."

"You, Hettie?"

"No, thank you, Mr. Spector. I'd prefer tea."

Bill, Hettie, and I shared anecdotes about newscast bloopers. Phil wowed us with tales about his trip with the Beatles on their first flight to the States from England.

"The boys laughed because I'm afraid of flying. Spent the entire flight pacing up and down the aisle," Phil said. "Ringo claimed I'm the only guy he knew who walked his way from Britain to America."

The party went on for hours. Phil orchestrated the room like a seasoned late-night talk show host—not an easy thing to do when you're surrounded by people who talk for a living. I forgot all about his crazy reputation, George's gun, and the hungry guard dogs. In another life, Phil could've been a stand-up comic.

The raucous mood stayed upbeat until we insisted it was time to go.

"You guys can't leave me now. It's only three a.m. for God's sake. The night is young." In seconds, Phil transformed from a gregarious music mogul to an abandoned lover from one of the many torch songs he'd produced. He lost his grin; his shoulders drooped. He looked well beyond his thirty-eight years. "Please stay."

His words hung in the air, waiting for someone—anyone—to collect them.

My entire adult life, I had seen Phil Spector as a legendary musical genius. Now, I had only pity for the guy. In front of me stood a sad, forlorn man scared to lose his audience, afraid to be alone. His pathetic plea played on our sympathy until we nearly reversed our decision. But I could tell by the look on Hettie's face that she'd had enough. And even though I was certain Bill and I could easily have been talked into staying longer, we bid our host a good night and headed out to the car.

I remember being filled with mixed emotions. One of my music idols was now just a guy in need of a friend. Did I want to be that friend? Would I care as much, if he wasn't Phil Spector? Was one night of this fast-lane lifestyle enough? Or was I ready for more?

As it turned out, Bill and I would return many times that spring for what we came to call *The Spector Show*. We had front-row seats for live performances several nights a week. Some nights it was comedy, other nights...drama. Whatever the genre, it was always entertaining and kept us returning to the mansion on the hill.

It got so, whenever the newsroom hotline rang shortly after nine at night, we knew it was him beckoning again. We had a choice: Spector or sleep. More often than not, Spector won.

Night after night, Hettie reminded us, "Be safe, boys."

Spring wore on, and I took to going to Spector's house without Bill. In a way, I think I wanted Spector all to myself. He'd become my recreational drug. I'd absorbed him into my veins and was always waiting for the next high. I could also score my next fix by hanging out with a multitude of music industry greats who would drop by to visit, or by overhearing late night phone calls Phil would take from famous musicians.

One night, John Lennon called. He was angry with Phil about something regarding a newspaper article and wouldn't stop shouting. It got so loud, I could hear both sides of the conversation. To this day, I don't know what article Lennon was referring to, but I'll never forget hearing the composer of "Imagine," "All You Need is Love," and "Give Peace a Chance" scream at the top of his lungs, "I tell you, it's bullshit, Phil. Fucking bullshit!"

Phil had significant history with The Beatles. He collaborated with Lennon on three legendary albums: *Let It Be*, *Imagine*, and *Plastic Ono Band*. One night, Phil proudly told me how he and John recorded the classic "Imagine" on a summer morning in Lennon's home studio. Phil also co-produced George Harrison's *All Things Must Pass* and *The Concert for Bangladesh*. I've always wondered if the phone conversation Phil had with Lennon that night was the last time he ever spoke with a Beatle.

Spector let many calls go straight to his answering machine, but he never turned down a chance to talk with a guy named Jerry Felder. Jerry would call from New York in the middle of the night. They'd chat about everything from politics to music to women.

One time, curiosity got the best of me. "Hey, Phil, who's this Jerry guy?"

"Jerry? I bet you know more about him than you think. In the business, he goes by Doc Pomus. He wrote classics like 'Save the Last Dance for Me' and 'This Magic Moment,' made famous by the Drifters. Jerry also wrote more than two dozen songs for Elvis: 'Viva Las Vegas,' 'Surrender,' and 'His Latest Flame.' If he'd had the voice and look, he could've been bigger than Elvis."

"If he's so talented, why does he stay huddled in his apartment and do nothin' but call you all the time?"

"I can't ignore his calls, Ken. Listen to the words of the song 'Save the Last Dance for Me.' He wrote it on his wedding day, as he watched his bride dance with every other man but him." Phil spoke softly as he removed a tear from his eye. "Jerry had polio as a kid and can't leave his wheelchair. When his wife later left him, he wrote 'Can't Get Used to Losing You.' The man breaks my heart."

I gained new insight that night into what made Phil tick. It was refreshing to see his human side. When it came down to it, I loved spending time with him.

Phil was infectious. He barely contained his laughter when he told me about the time he paid the mercurial Ike Turner twenty thousand dollars to stay out of the studio while his wife, Tina, recorded the song "River Deep, Mountain High." And he loved sharing the story of how he recruited everyone from Cher to Glen Campbell to sing backup on the Righteous Brothers' song "You've Lost That Lovin' Feeling." Contrary to his instinct about the song, everyone thought it was too long and too slow to be a hit. That record ended up getting more radio airtime than any other song in the twentieth century. The man was pure genius.

At times, I had the honor of joining in on sing-alongs that featured Phil on the Steinway piano and me, the whitest white guy you've ever seen, doing my best Marvin Gaye imitations. Trust me, it wasn't pretty.

All in all, I felt special around the guy. I was close enough to him to share intimate thoughts about my career, my relationships, and life in general. He made me feel part of his inner circle—a feeling, I admit, that was immensely seductive. Here I was, in the midst of spectacular opulence, hanging out with one of my rock-and-roll heroes who treated me like a trusted confidant.

But, more and more, there were signs that madness lurked inside the maestro.

"Everybody arm yourselves. Let's form a posse!" Phil said to George and me one night. Across town, some thugs had injured his mother when they'd snatched her purse. Phil was so determined to track down the bad guys, I could practically see his words explode into flaming embers as they left his mouth.

"We're gonna kill the Nazi pricks who did this!"

It took everything we had to keep Phil from forcing us to join him for a lynching, but, in time, George talked him out of it. The incident, however, revealed a lot about Phil's hotheaded, impulsive nature.

I also came to expect sharp mood changes in direct relation to how much booze he'd tossed back. I never knew what was really going on in the clogged canals of Phil's tortured mind. One minute, he'd joke about his favorite comedian, Lenny Bruce, then he'd burst into tears talking about his father's suicide. Phil's dad took his life when Phil was only nine. The title of the first hit record Phil wrote, "To Know Him Is to Love Him," is taken from the words on his father's tombstone.

With each new erratic incident, I'd see another troubled facet of him, compounding the notion that maybe I was in over my head.

So why did I continue to hang out with a man whose mental state lay somewhere between slightly off-kilter and batshit crazy? I'm not sure I know the answer, but, over the years, I've come up with three possible reasons.

First, I was a fearless kid in my early twenties, with no steady girlfriend to tie me down, and was highly susceptible to temptation.

Second, news people by nature are excitement junkies, risk takers, and a little nuts, themselves, so it was natural for me to be drawn to Phil's brand of crazy.

And third, this was frickin' Phil Spector, rock icon and the very first celebrity I had the opportunity to regard as a personal friend. I'd be lying if I said it wasn't a major ego stroke.

One rainy evening, while we played pinball in his game room, Phil confided he was secretly working on his first album in several years; he was nervous about it, since his last one flopped. He wanted to go in an entirely new direction and surprise a lot of folks. He was more excited than I'd seen him in weeks.

"Gonna collaborate with Leonard Cohen," he whispered in my ear. "Ever heard of him?"

"Uh, yeah!"

Not only had I heard of him, the Canadian folk singer and master poet had been a favorite of mine ever since I first heard his classic songs, "Suzanne," "Bird on a Wire," and "So Long, Marianne," in college. A true modern Renaissance man.

Leonard Cohen (Courtesy: Gorup-de-Besanez)

But Spector and Cohen? That's like Manilow and Mozart—not exactly a match made in heaven. I was sure Leonard's intimate, intellectual, and largely minimalist interpretation of the human condition would be crushed by Spector's Wagnerian Wall of Sound.

"What are you gonna call it?" I asked.

"Leonard and I agreed on *Death of a Ladies' Man*. Nice ring to it, don't ya think?"

I wasn't sure what to think, but who was I to question a guy who'd sold countless millions of records? About a week later, Bill and I were among a handful of guests invited to the album's first recording session.

We drove to Hollywood's Gold Star Studios and found the nondescript building in an area of Tinseltown the Chamber of Commerce doesn't want you to know about. Frightening faces, crowded liquor stores, and decrepit hotels of questionable repute dotted the landscape. Both Bill and I had covered our share of gang shootings in the area.

Yet, despite its shady surroundings, we learned from Phil that Gold Star was the site of more music history than almost any recording studio in the world. Upon entering, I swear I could feel the presence of legendary artists who'd made history there: John Lennon, Neil Young, the Beach Boys, Jimi Hendrix, the Who, Tina Turner, the Association, and the Righteous Brothers, to name a few. Even Ronald Reagan and Marlon Brando recorded voice-over tracks there.

In true Spector style, Phil scheduled the recording session to go all night and set the studio thermometer on icy cold to keep everybody awake. Musicians tuned their instruments, cigarette smoke filled the air, and excitement permeated every corner of the place.

The best studio musicians in the business packed the room to capacity. Known as the Wrecking Crew, their credits included hundreds of hit records, film scores, and commercials. But most people never knew it was them making the music. Early Wrecking Crew members like Glen Campbell and Leon Russell went on to stardom, but the majority lived in relative obscurity while they made others rich and famous.

The album *Pet Sounds* is a great example. Many think it's the Beach Boys' finest work. But it's the Wrecking Crew who came up with many of the licks and played most of those instruments you hear.

The Monkees? Davy, Michael, Mickey, and Peter garnered all the attention, but the Wrecking Crew provided those catchy tunes on their early albums.

"Mr. Tambourine Man?" Most would say it was performed by the Byrds, but they'd be only partially correct. Just one Byrd (Roger McGuinn) actually played on the record. All the other instruments were played by...the Wrecking Crew.

On this particular night, the Crew gathered to record the song, "Don't Go Home with Your Heart On."

As I soaked in the energy of the place, I sensed an imposing male figure over my left shoulder. When I turned to look, his black fedora, rumpled sport coat, and buttoned shirt gave the aura of a contented college professor. To my surprise, I found myself inches away from the distinctive voice that had gotten me through broken romances and late-night study sessions in college.

"Hey there. You a friend of Phil's?"

Leonard Cohen's earthy baritone sounded like a Cape Cod foghorn in a midnight thunderstorm, but his Canadian humility shined through his hazel eyes and welcoming smile. As we came face-to-face, I tried my best to act nonchalant, even though my heart was pounding.

"Yes. Phil invited my buddy Bill and me to tag along. It's a tremendous honor to meet you, Mr. Cohen."

Just as I was wishing I'd come up with a more intellectual response, Phil intervened and invited us over to meet the background singers. They included renowned beat generation poet Allen Ginsburg and a guy with a frumpy hat and dark glasses who looked somewhat familiar.

"Guys, wantcha to meet Bobby Zimmerman," Phil said.

I realized right away I was shaking the hand of Bob Dylan (Zimmerman is his real last name). He looked like a panhandler and smelled like a smokestack, but I didn't care. There I stood, opposite one of the most influential artists of my generation.

No doubt a special night lay ahead.

Phil ruled the recording studio like a dictator, commanding the musicians to record take after take, sometimes for well over an hour, till they played a bar of notes to his complete satisfaction.

"Cut. Cut! You blew it again. I told you the drum comes in a half-beat before the piano. Take twelve."

Cohen and Ginsberg hung out in the recording portion of the studio while Bill and I sat on a couch in the control room, right behind Phil and his engineer, Larry Levine. Dylan read a paperback in the corner, oblivious to his surroundings. No big deal to him—he'd seen a thousand recording sessions.

My thoughts were focused on the prospect of talking to Dylan. When it came time for a break, I got up the nerve to approach the music legend. As I did, my conscience attempted to stonewall me: *Better not screw this up. Failure is not an option.*

"Uh, Mr. Dylan, I was wondering if I could ask you a question."

"*Errg*, whoddia? Whudja wun frumee? Blergghhh."

At least I think that's what Dylan said. I can't be sure, since he mumbled in a voice that sounded like he gargled with gravel. I pretended to understand and persevered. "Uh, I'm a television producer and would love to produce a two-hour special on your incredible life."

Dylan's answer may as well have been blowin' in the wind, because, this time, I couldn't comprehend a single syllable. Whatever he said, I sensed the matter should be dropped and humbly returned to my place on the velvet couch.

I'm an idiot. Why would Bob Dylan want to have anything to do with me?

Around midnight, Phil sent for pizza—lots of pizza. He ordered something like twenty boxes of every variety imaginable plus enough garlic bread to feed a small army.

When the grub arrived, the Wrecking Crew proceeded to embark on a feeding frenzy. Among those binging on bread and pounding down pepperoni were:

Hal Blaine, who is widely regarded as the most recorded drummer in history, with fifty number-one hits to his credit. That's his signature beat at the beginning of "Be My Baby" by The Ronettes and his crashing percussion at the end of "Bridge over Troubled Water" by Simon and Garfunkel.

Don Randi, who has backed up everybody from Frank Sinatra to Frank Zappa. You can hear him playing the piano on "Good Vibrations" and "God Only Knows" by The Beach Boys as well as the harpsichord on "Different Drum" by Linda Ronstadt.

And Steve Douglas, who has recorded with Aretha, Elvis, and Cher just to mention a few. His wailing saxophone is featured on the soundtracks of dozens of movies, from *One Flew Over the Cuckoo's Nest* to *Fast Times at Ridgemont High*.

If a bomb had gone off in the studio, the music industry would've been set back at least a half century. Mercifully, that didn't happen, but I did see something that could've instantly sent any one of us to the Promised Land. While Phil bent over to grab a bite of pizza, his jacket fell open to display a gold-plated revolver in his waistband. One of the guitarists noticed me eye Phil's weapon.

"Don't worry." He laughed. "Phil is all show."

I could only hope he was right.

Around two in the morning, the time came to record background vocals. Phil told Dylan and Ginsburg to go to the microphones in the studio. Then he turned to Bill and me.

"Gentlemen, I hope you're in fine voice tonight."

I nearly choked on my pizza. *Phil Spector wants me to*

sing? I can't carry a tune in a bucket with two handles.

Bill was fine with it—he sang lead in several rock bands before taking up broadcasting. Me? I'd always made a point of confining my singing to the shower. But the tug on my ego to sing alongside Bob Dylan and Leonard Cohen was greater than the obvious fact I had no business doing so.

Bill stood with me next to Dylan and Ginsburg as we prepared to give it our best shot. The plan called for Leonard to sing, "When you called, she was always there…" Then the four of us would repeat his words in unison. *How hard could it be?* I reasoned.

A hush fell over the studio.

"Take one, roll music, ready vocals," Phil said from the control room.

On cue, we began singing the repeated words, "When you called…"

"Cut. Cut! A little flat guys. Once more."

"When you called, she was always…"

"Cut. Cut! It's still not right. Take three."

This went on so many times, I lost count. Dylan and Ginsburg looked bored. Phil came out of the control room and strolled up to me.

"Ken, got a special job for you. Why don't you step over to this other microphone?"

Today, if you look on YouTube for "Don't Go Home with Your Heart On," my record debut begins ten seconds into the song. You can hear me…clapping to the beat. Sadly, for some reason, my talented handiwork isn't credited on the album.

The recording session wrapped at dawn, along with any hopes I had of being the next Marvin Gaye. I felt deflated at night's end. I knew I couldn't sing well, but I did want to at least make a good impression. Everyone else felt that sense of accomplishment after a hard night's work; the first song on the album was completed. As for me, I had to take comfort in the mere fact that, throughout a tension-filled night, Phil never felt the need to use his gun.

As spring turned into summer, the recording sessions took on a more ominous tone. Phil's behavior changed. He bounced to the beat of an agitated song no one else could hear. He grew more and more impatient. A college professor once told me you can gauge the substance of a man by how he treats his subordinates. By that measure, Phil didn't even move the needle.

I managed as well as possible to lie low as he berated everyone around him like a paranoid dictator sensing he was about to be overthrown. He couldn't be pleased. The drums were too loud, the vocals too flat, the temperature too warm, and the food too cold. A constant fury burned in his eyes—the same fury I saw when he reacted to his mother being attacked. Phil had climbed onboard the crazy train and it was clear no one could stop it.

Before long, he went off the rails.

Late one night, after I'd gone home, I'm told Phil staggered toward Leonard with a bottle of wine in one hand and a shiny object in the other. He wrapped his arm around Leonard's shoulder then shoved a .45 revolver into the singer's neck.

"Leonard, I love you," Phil said.

According to those who were there, Leonard's brow crinkled as his eyes reached to look at the gun in his neck. He seemed puzzled, then annoyed. Leonard pushed Phil's arm away, saying, "I hope you do, Phil."

Though Leonard survived Phil's momentary insanity, their friendship and celebrated collaboration came to a thunderous halt. Phil barred Leonard from the final recording session and mixed the album by himself.

That incident at the recording studio cemented any concerns I had about hanging out with Phil. I didn't know this man anymore and wondered if I ever had.

I decided, in order to literally survive my twenties and maintain some semblance of pride in the process, I'd have to end my association with Phil. But rather than cut him off cold turkey, I held out for a swan song. I asked Phil if I could invite two longtime pals to his mansion. Both were musicians, anxious to meet Spector for themselves. Phil gave the okay.

Late one Saturday night, I showed up with my buddies Chris Tripoli and Richard Walker. Phil met us, drink in hand, with a thin, beautiful blonde in a slinky black dress by his side. Both were decked out for a night on the town. George, as always, quietly stood guard.

"Tonight, we're going to the Hong Kong Bar in Century City to hear Barney and Herb perform," Phil said. Barney Kessel and Herb Ellis were highly respected jazz guitarists. Kessel was a charter member of the Wrecking Crew.

Phil ordered a limousine and drinks for everyone then turned to my friends.

"Who are you guys again? Why the hell are you here?"

"Come on, Phil. They're my buddies," I said. "Remember, you told me I could bring 'em over."

"They're lookin' at me weird, makin' me nervous."

Phil glared at my friends, spit out his drink, then reached for his waistband like he was going for his gun.

My buddies looked at me in disbelief. Phil's date took three steps back.

"We just wanted to meet ya, Phil," my pal Richard said.

"We don't want any trouble," Chris said.

The limo arrived, and Phil and George went out to meet

the driver. I thought this would break the tension.

I was dead wrong.

"Get off my property now or I'll kill you!" Phil shouted as he pointed his pistol at the limo driver. "I'm not fuckin' around. This gun is loaded."

The ashen-faced driver gunned the gas, raced down the driveway, and sped into the night.

Phil spun around toward George. "The guy's a fake. He's really from *The National Enquirer*. Bastard was gonna try and take my picture."

Phil then pointed his gun at my buddies and me in the entryway.

He moved toward Richard. "You're a goddamn junkie."

Then he aimed his pistol at Chris. "And you're a narc. It's no coincidence you guys showed up the same night as that *Enquirer* photographer."

Chris and Richard were speechless, the skin on their faces pale as death.

I'm not sure what Phil's deranged mind thought my connection was to all this, but I'll never forget when he slowly turned and pointed his gun at me.

I froze. No time to run, no place to hide. No chance to say goodbye to my parents, my sister, my friends.

Phil kept moving closer and closer. My eyes focused on every detail of the .38 snub-nose in his trembling hand—the black gun barrel, the shiny bullet chamber, his shaky finger on the silver trigger. Never would I have guessed, after all we'd been through, Phil Spector would have me at gunpoint.

I clenched my teeth and closed my eyes. All I could do was wait for a bullet to penetrate my brain.

CHAPTER 3
ON THE ROAD AGAIN

GRIPPING THE STEERING wheel until my fingers turned purple, I drove along a scenic section of Mulholland Drive overlooking Hollywood. It had been a full twenty-four hours since Phil Spector came within inches of blowing my brains out, but my hands were still shaking.

Thank God George grabbed Phil's arm and talked sense into the walking time bomb before he could pull the trigger. Instinct told me to crouch low and run toward the darkness, to make myself a more difficult target. I'll never know if Spector planned to shoot me, but I'm forever grateful I didn't have to find out.

That night at the Spector mansion was the last time I ever saw Phil. I felt betrayed. My admiration turned to anger and disgust. Everyone, including me, had given Phil a break because of who he was. But he wasn't worth our respect. He called me several times, asking me to stop by, but I valued my life too much to ever see him again.

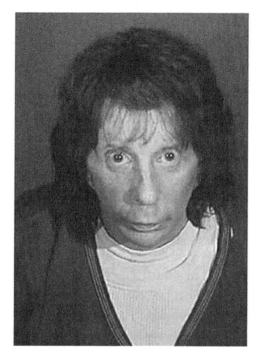

Phil Spector (Courtesy: LAPD)

Good thing I didn't. Years later, Phil was convicted of murdering actress Lana Clarkson in a drunken show of misguided manhood. Although he had moved twenty miles away to a castle in Alhambra, the situation was eerily similar to what my friends and I experienced. I made my share of bad choices in my youth, but my decision to stop seeing Phil Spector wasn't one of them. It may have saved my life.

I'd always done my clearest thinking while driving, so this was the perfect time to make some weighty decisions about my young life. Having a loaded gun pointed to your head tends to make you re-evaluate your priorities. Hell, it can make you instantly find religion. I knew I was done with Phil, but was I done with the bewitching world of broadcasting, as well?

I was only twenty-six but had already experienced a lifetime of colorful characters with inflated egos and questionable ethics. One time, a few years earlier, when I was disc jockey at KUPD in Phoenix, my boss took over my show and ordered me to score some marijuana for him from my college buddies. I was stunned and pretended to try but came back empty. Another time, when I was an anchorman in Flagstaff, the inebriated station owner threatened to "f**king fire me" if I didn't lead the news with a positive story about President Nixon—a difficult order at the height of Watergate. Under pressure, I copped out and reported some unimportant story about Nixon at a charity ball.

As I continued driving along Mulholland, I wondered if I'd taken a wrong turn in judgment somewhere along the way. Was having a loaded gun pointed at my head a sign from above? Not much of a churchgoer, I did at least believe in a higher power, so I asked the big guy what He thought.

"Excuse me, God. Are you telling me I'm not cut out for this industry? You trying to tell me I should join the respectable world of education, like everyone else in my family?"

God didn't give me a straight answer. But I thought I heard Him reply words to the effect of, "Maybe so, Ken, but for now, just keep your eyes on the road."

And that's what I did. I kept my eyes on the road, hoping to see signs that would send me down the right path.

My seductress, however, was far from done with me. She remained in the shadows enough so I could sense her presence, which, any red-blooded male will tell you, makes the sweet scent of seduction even stronger. Truth be told, late at night, when my twilight dreams were more honest than my daytime intentions, I knew I wanted at least one more dance with her—on the *national* stage. Radio and local TV stations are one thing, but the hallowed halls of the networks are quite another.

It wasn't long before my dream came true. I received a job offer from the big boys. Not a network, but the next best thing: KNXT (now KCBS), the CBS Network flagship station in Los Angeles. They wanted an assignment editor—the person who helps decide what stories are covered and then dispatches reporters and camera crews to the scene. KNXT had plans to expand their early evening news from one hour to a groundbreaking two-and-a-half hours, and they needed able bodies to staff it, pronto.

This was the station where Johnny Carson got his start in TV and James Dean once worked as an usher. The building was a monument to the history of twentieth century media. The pilot episode of *I Love Lucy* was shot there. Bob Hope, George Burns, and Jack Benny made audiences howl with laughter there. Barbra Streisand, Simon & Garfunkel, and Janis Joplin were among the music greats who recorded classic albums there.

I immediately said yes to the job offer.

KNXT ruled the marketplace when I was growing up. *The Big News*, anchored by Jerry Dunphy, was so big, it had more viewers than all other Southern California newscasts combined. But, in 1975, a dimwitted KNXT executive deemed Dunphy too old to attract younger viewers (he had reached the *ancient* age of fifty-four), so he was unceremoniously let go. Literally within hours, ABC's local station, KABC, hired Dunphy and patted themselves on their backs as their ratings skyrocketed. It was the local news equivalent of when the Boston Red Sox traded away Babe Ruth to the New York Yankees. It's rumored that the executive who fired Dunphy ended up selling used cars in Barstow.

Meanwhile, NBC's local station, KNBC, gained ground with a stable of local stars, including Paul Moyer, Kelly Lange, Bryant Gumble, Jess Marlow, and future game-show host Pat Sajak, who at the time was doing the weather. When I arrived on scene, in the late seventies, KNXT's newscasts were a distant third in the ratings.

Seeking to spark new life into their valuable L.A. affiliate, CBS whipped out their corporate wallet and recruited some heavyweights:

Connie Chung received a healthy chunk of change to leave her network-correspondent gig and become KNXT's newest anchorwoman. Brent Musberger stepped up to the plate from CBS Network's sports division to provide some punch to the lineup. Pat O'Brien came from Chicago, where his unorthodox reporting style at WMAQ-TV helped garner big ratings in the Midwest. Pat had a reputation for being a high-maintenance wise-ass, but his on-camera skills more than made up for any flaws in personality. KNXT enticed him with a leased Mercedes and a boatload of per diem money.

CBS made sure to keep veterans like Ralph Story, Bill Stout, and Jim Hill, and to promote rising stars like Linda Douglass, Roy Firestone, and Steve Edwards as they prepared to launch the nation's longest local TV newscast.

They also hired new behind-the-scenes producers, writers, and me—a kid from Altadena who was convinced he was ready to play in the big leagues. Despite my trepidations about the egos, ethics, and instability of the broadcasting world, my enchantress effortlessly hooked me in again.

My first day on the job set the stage for what was to

come at KNXT. I parked in the same lot where I pictured James Dean used to rev his engine, and then proudly obtained my name badge from the security guard and opened the door that led into the newsroom. I immediately encountered a familiar, well-worn face barking opinions at a younger man through a cloud of cigarette smoke.

"Let the bastard rot in prison! Why the hell should we give him air time?"

I had no idea what Bill Stout was talking about, but I did know the legendary curmudgeon was a force to be reckoned with. Stout had been one of the most respected television journalists in the biz for decades and had even filled in for Walter Cronkite back in the day. He spoke his mind, no matter what the consequences. Everybody knew: B.S. took no BS.

I did my best to get out of Stout's way and took in the dynamic view behind him. Straight ahead lay a massive sea of desks, populated by writers and producers. Off to my right, a flashy news set put the anchors in the heart of the action. Toward the center looked like mission control. A man spoke into a two-way radio, surrounded by folks at a circular desk. He was the on-duty assignment editor, encircled by fervent production assistants, all busy researching breaking news stories. The back wall consisted of a series of edit bays where sharp minds and nimble fingers put the pictures and sound together.

Eager, jovial, good-looking faces were everywhere, but this was only a small portion of the news team. Elsewhere in the bustling building were the investigative unit, the story planning department, the film and tape library, and areas for sports, weather, entertainment, engineering, and graphics, as well as offices for reporters and management. And this was just the first floor. Upstairs, KNX Radio blanketed the West Coast with news coverage around the clock. It takes a small town to report big-city news.

I smiled as I took it all in. A major commitment to journalism. Fresh energy. Lots of pretty women. My kind of place.

I was thrown right into the fire my first week on the job. It was my task to assign a reporter to cover a shooting in the crime-ridden city of Compton. I chose Jim Giggans.

Jim was a proud African-American man who let everyone know he lived in Beverly Hills, attended the opera, and was fluent in several languages. In fact, when he didn't want someone to overhear his phone conversation, he would often speak French to retain privacy.

"I hope you're not sending me there just because I'm black," Jim said after I radioed him the address. He was obviously sensitive about the assignment and didn't want to be pigeonholed. Being the new guy on the block, the last thing I wanted to do was tick him off.

"Never crossed my mind, Jim," I truthfully replied. "You just happen to be the closest reporter to the scene."

Major market newsrooms tend to attract as many outlandish characters as a convention of professional wrestlers. KNXT was no exception, so I took pains to understand the players. For instance, Connie Chung took pride in her politically incorrect sense of humor. This I realized when she said to me, "You know, we Asians have a slanted view of the news." I didn't know whether to laugh or pretend I was deaf.

Roy Firestone

In addition to being a first-class sportscaster, Roy Firestone did the funniest impressions of anyone I've ever heard. You haven't lived until you've heard his dead-on versions of Frank Sinatra belting out "YMCA" or Muhammad Ali fighting with Howard Cosell. To this day, he performs his act in front of sold-out audiences around the world.

Weekend anchorman Ken Jones loved the ponies and spent much of his free time at the racetrack. Depending on how his bets turned out, he would either strut around the newsroom, flashing hundred dollar bills, or hit up his co-workers for lunch money.

Then there was Pat O'Brien. He was arrogant, caustic, and, by his own admission, snorted an insane amount of cocaine—up to $2,000 a week in today's money. I guess that's where he spent his boatload of per diem money.

Everybody ignored Pat's behavior, knowing full well he was the finest TV reporter in town. Whether it was an investigation into the use of excessive force by the LAPD, unearthing the details of the Guyana massacre orchestrated by cult leader Jim Jones, or digging into the story behind the untimely death of John Lennon, he got the big stories and did us proud. In fact, pride ran rampant at 6121 Sunset Boulevard in Hollywood. Our profession became our passion.

I quickly moved up the ranks at KNXT and, after just a few months, found myself doing everything from writing lead stories to working in the field on some of the biggest news stories of the day and even occasionally producing for a creative new feature show called *2 on the Town.*

Diggin' life with my pal Darryl Meathe back in the day

I first became infatuated with the art of storytelling when my dad produced plays starring the neighborhood kids and, later, when my lifelong friend Darryl Meathe and I filmed amateur movies in high school. I couldn't believe that, at KNXT, I was earning good money doing something I loved. Much like my early visits to Phil Spector's mansion, I looked forward to spending my time at the building known as Columbia Square.

I had my share of memorable experiences at KNXT, but two will forever haunt me.

The *first* was when I was sent north to produce a story about an up-and-coming politician named Harvey Milk. Harvey, as he insisted I call him, was a San Francisco County Supervisor who was leading the fight against a controversial initiative on the California ballot known as Proposition Six. Sponsored by conservative Orange County lawmaker John Briggs, it aimed to ban gays and lesbians from teaching in the state's public schools.

I spent several days with Harvey leading up to the election. The experience was a real eye-opener. For the first time in my life, I became friends with an openly gay man. Like many others, I'd interacted with people with different sexual orientations my entire life but had been completely naïve about that fact. Now, I was hanging out with the man they called "The Mayor of Castro Street," arguably the gayest neighborhood in the country. Harvey knew I was straight and may even have been amused by my naïveté, but he treated me like a brother as we dined, drank, and attended campaign rallies.

On election night, I felt satisfaction in watching Harvey rejoice when Proposition Six was soundly defeated. I returned home happy and, just as importantly, with an enlightened perspective on a lifestyle very different from mine, yet in so many ways very much the same.

Ten days later, I heard these frenetic words blast from the office loudspeaker: *"San Francisco Mayor George Moscone and Supervisor Harvey Milk have just been assassinated!"*

My heart sank. I rushed to the assignment desk, hoping there had been some mistake.

There hadn't.

(Courtesy: San Francisco Chronicle)

Former San Francisco County Supervisor Dan White had murdered Harvey and Mayor Moscone in cold blood over a political grudge. Dianne Feinstein, then president of the Board of Supervisors, discovered their bodies after hearing gunshots inside City Hall.

I decided to leave work early that day. Anyone who tells you journalists aren't personally affected by the news either doesn't know what the hell they're talking about or is a liar.

The *second* experience that still haunts me from my KNXT days is about one of the most notorious killing sprees in the history of Southern California.

CHAPTER 4
STRANGLERS IN THE NIGHT

LOS ANGELES IS BIG—so big you can fit Boston, San Francisco, Pittsburgh, Saint Louis, Minneapolis, Cleveland, Milwaukee, and the entire island of Manhattan within its borders. And that's just the incorporated part. The metro area could house a small country. Author Dorothy Parker supposedly once said, "Los Angeles is seventy-two suburbs in search of a city."

But when the Hillside Strangler started killing young women, it didn't take much for the City of Angels to feel like a small town in Iowa. It seemed like everyone united in fear.

For an addicted news junkie like me, the story was made-to-order. A killer on the loose, a city under siege, and it was all happening in my own backyard. Before it was over, I became closer to the story than I ever could have imagined.

October 1977

The lifeless body of Yolanda Washington was found on the slopes of the distinguished Forest Lawn Cemetery near Hollywood. The twenty-year-old prostitute had marks around her neck, wrists, and ankles where she'd been bound by a rope. It barely made the news. Another day, another murder in L.A.

Two weeks later, a homeowner discovered the strangled remains of fifteen-year-old Judith Lynn Miller in the hilly suburb of La Crescenta. Like the first victim, she'd been bound with rope and raped. Both had obviously been killed elsewhere, wiped clean of prints, and left out in the open to be easily found.

Five days later, aspiring ballerina Lissa Kastin was found strangled to death on a hill overlooking a Glendale country club. The ambitious twenty-one-year-old worked as a waitress at night to fund her aspirations. When she bid goodbye to her co-workers the night before, they had no way of knowing it would be her final farewell.

Three young women, tortured and strangled with ropes, cleaned of prints, then callously dumped on public hillsides as if to taunt police. Detectives knew this was no coincidence. Southern Californians began to whisper seven words no one wants to hear: *A serial killer is on the loose.*

I admit, those of us in the media did all we could to whip the community into a frenzy. To make the story juicier, we made sure the killer had a catchy moniker. Soon, the name *Hillside Strangler* blared out of newscasts and headlines.

Whether the killer felt encouraged by the news coverage or was simply following an original plan, the sadistic streak continued. The following week, two girls, ages twelve and fourteen, went missing. Dolores Cepeda and Sonja Johnson were last seen getting into a car outside an Eagle Rock mall. Police didn't connect them to the other crimes until their strangled bodies were found on a trash-strewn hillside near Dodger Stadium.

A few hours later, a sixth victim turned up on a Glendale

hillside. Twenty-year-old Kristina Weckler was not only strangled and sexually assaulted, but her body had been injected with Windex. Police were dealing with a real sicko.

Fear hung in the air like a flammable gas. Women were scared for their lives, even afraid to be stopped for a traffic violation since there was speculation the killer or killers pretended to be police officers. Men were concerned about the safety of their girlfriends, wives, and daughters.

Then, the first break in the case: a witness came forward who said he saw the twelve- and fourteen-year-old victims get into a car with two men inside—a piece of information that seemed to align with the detectives' growing belief that it would take at least two people to move the bodies to the hilly locations where they were found. What stumped them was that, historically, serial killers rarely worked in pairs.

Three days after the witness came forward, the badly decomposed remains of twenty-eight-year-old actress Jane King were discovered near an off-ramp of the Golden State Freeway in the Los Feliz area. Victim number seven. That really hit home for me, since it was an exit I took every day on my drive to work in Hollywood. Like many of the other victims, her body had been posed in a grotesque position.

Less than a week later, the severely tortured body of Lauren Wagner was found across the street from her parents' home in the San Fernando Valley. Another break— a neighbor saw the eighteen-year-old high school student arguing with two men before getting into a dark car with them.

I lived in Altadena during those unnerving days, only a few miles from many of the crime scenes. While on the job at KNXT, I'd write news stories about the crimes with a calm, if not cool, professionalism befitting the job. But at home, I became as rattled as anyone else. Who will be the next victim? Where will she be found? Will it be someone I know?

The Los Angeles Police Department, the Los Angeles County Sheriff's Department, and the Glendale Police Department combined to form the Hillside Strangler Task Force. But, in this era before DNA testing, clues were few and far between.

Just about everyone I knew channeled their inner Columbo:

> *Were the killers real police officers using their badges of authority to lure victims?*

> *Most of the bodies were scrubbed clean, as if being prepared for surgery. Did one of the killers have a medical background?*

> *Were these guys part of a bigger, cold-blooded cult conducting sadistic initiations?*

Nobody knew the answers, least of all me. All I or anyone could say for sure was... the nightmare wasn't over.

Two weeks after the discovery of Lauren Wagner's body, police discovered victim number nine. Seventeen-year-old Kimberly Martin was found strangled on a steep hillside near downtown Los Angeles. Another clue: investigators determined the killer had lured her from a pay phone in the lobby of the Hollywood Public Library.

By this point, the killing spree had consumed most of the autumn season, but it ceased with an eerie lull when winter arrived. Christmas came. New Year's. Valentine's Day. Many people thought maybe, just maybe, the killings had stopped.

They were wrong.

February 1978

A helicopter pilot spotted an orange Datsun abandoned off a cliff on Angeles Crest Highway, north of the city. In the trunk, they found the strangled, violated body of twenty-one-year-old Cindy Hudspeth. The vivacious store clerk, who gave dance lessons to earn money for college, had apparently been kidnapped from outside her Glendale apartment. Another possible clue: she lived across the street from victim Kristina Weckler, but the two women apparently hadn't known each other.

Southern California rallied around a singular goal: the killings must stop.

And they did.

Spring ushered in summer. Summer eased into fall. The winter holidays came and went, and the Strangler remained quiet. Talk returned to how the Dodgers and Lakers were doing. Radios blared the latest songs from Rod Stewart and Fleetwood Mac. Even the Hillside Strangler Task Force disbanded.

But thoughts of the snuffed-out lives of ten young women remained in the back of everyone's mind...

Did the "monster" discover a conscience? Did it realize it would have to answer to a higher authority? Did it suffer the same fate as its victims?

Many of us hoped all three of those possibilities were true.

January 1979

A crime occurred twelve hundred miles to the north of Los Angeles that blew the Hillside Strangler case wide open.

Two Western Washington University coeds were found raped and strangled in Bellingham, Washington. Karen Mandic and Diane Wilder thought they were applying for a housesitting job when they were attacked. Police found them in the trunk of Mandic's abandoned car.

It didn't take long for the authorities to solve the murders. Officers discovered a piece of paper in Mandic's car with the name "Kenneth Bianchi."

The twenty-seven-year-old's fingerprints were found, as well. When police located and arrested him, they learned Bianchi previously lived in the Glendale area during the siege of the Strangler. He even lived in the same apartment building as one of the girls who was murdered. When they searched his house, they found the clincher: jewelry that belonged to several of the Southern California victims.

Bianchi knew the evidence against him was overwhelming, so he did everything he could to avoid prosecution. At first, he feigned multiple personalities to support an insanity defense. But a shrewd psychiatrist exposed the ruse.

Bianchi ditched the insanity defense. He came up with a new plan to avoid a visit to the gas chamber. He claimed there were *two* Hillside Stranglers. In an attempt to avoid the death penalty, he was willing to testify against his alleged partner in crime, Angelo Buono.

Police detectives had no problem finding Buono. He was Bianchi's older cousin and ran an auto upholstery shop next to his home on Colorado Boulevard in Glendale — right in the heart of Strangler country. Six miles to the east, Colorado Boulevard is classy, best known for hosting the world-famous Tournament of Roses Parade in Pasadena and for being the home of Vroman's, the oldest and largest independent bookstore in Southern California. But this portion of the boulevard held no such glamour, populated as it was by old neighborhood bars, rundown apartments, and Buono's seemingly ordinary upholstery shop. Police hauled him in for questioning, but, of course, he denied everything. Since Bianchi was an unreliable witness, Buono remained free.

All the while, at KNXT, I'd been chomping at the bit, hungry for a chance to break in big on this story, to make a name for myself. A journalist needs a nugget to work with, and I finally had mine. The problem was—so did my counterparts at every other news outlet.

The time had come to step up my game.

If I wanted to rise above my competitors, I'd have to devote every waking hour to learn what I could about Buono, the forty-four-year-old son of Italian immigrants. The more I knew, the closer I could position myself to either observe him or even interact with him.

I learned Buono had a long criminal history ranging from grand theft auto to assault. But, despite his shady past, he ran what appeared to be a successful business. I talked with random people in his neighborhood and found out that Rolls Royces were often parked outside Buono's shop. His clients included Frank Sinatra and a vocalist with the Supremes. At least, that's what he bragged to his neighbors. I also learned a juicy tidbit that I suspected could prove valuable later on: the location of his favorite neighborhood bar. I caught a buzz just thinking about it.

But according to those who knew him—as best as one can know a potentially unexposed serial killer—Buono's interests went beyond car upholstery and booze. He loved being surrounded by young women. Prior to his name surfacing in the Hillside Strangler case, teenage girls were often seen frequenting his shop. He proudly called himself "The Italian Stallion," something I'm sure Sylvester Stallone would've shuddered to know. But some neighbors had a hunch more than virility was involved. They suspected he ran a prostitution ring.

The more I learned, the greater the allure of the chase. I hadn't done this kind of investigation before and found myself completely submerged in it. Of course, all the media outlets had his house and shop staked out, but back then I only had five or six competitors. That was a good thing. Today, there would be six news vans, three helicopters, and two drones. And, in the midst of the chaos, a perfectly coiffed Anderson Cooper would be hosting his CNN show live at the scene.

Occasionally, some brave soul would knock on Buono's door, but no one answered. Outside his shop, a sign read: *Temporarily Closed.* Someone I know even went through Buono's mail in search of clues—entirely unethical in the business, and yet I suspect he wasn't the only one who stooped so low. Everybody was trying to nail this guy.

I had a distinct advantage over many of the other journalists. Most of them went home to their wives, girlfriends, or family as soon as their news shift ended. I had nobody in particular in my life at the time, so I was more than willing to work after hours on my own time—with or without a camera crew.

Late one chilly Saturday night, when the workweek was done for most folks, I drove past Buono's place, looking for signs of life. The only other broadcaster around was a young, friendly guy named Judd Rose. Judd, like me, was at the beginning of his career—a rookie radio reporter for local station KFWB. Many years later, he would go on to win four Emmys as an investigative reporter for ABC News and co-anchor for CNN.

Judd and I hit it off right away. We sat in my car across the street from Buono's upholstery shop and swapped Strangler stories as well as our theories about the "Italian Stallion." Since we didn't work for direct competitors, we felt free sharing a few things we'd each learned about the case.

"Ken, I think the neighbors may know more than they're telling police."

"You've got my full attention, Judd."

"A lady came up to me on the street. Told me she heard what sounded like a girl's screams coming from Buono's house last year."

"Did she tell the cops?"

"I don't know, but I doubt it. When I tried to get her to say more, her husband told her to shut up then rushed her away."

I locked eyes with Judd. "Interesting. That could be enough to get the slimeball arrested."

"I just wish I knew which apartment they live in. I lost them in the night."

The only information I had to offer Judd was the location of Buono's favorite watering hole. I knew this tidbit was important, but something had kept me from following through on the lead earlier. Could've been the prospect of venturing alone into the belly of the beast.

"Maybe that's where his neighbors hang out on Saturday nights," I said.

Judd paused a beat then displayed a devious grin. "You know, I'm kinda thirsty. What do ya say we go get ourselves a drink?"

"You read my mind," I replied.

We drove down the street and into the bar's parking lot. From the outside, it looked typical of almost any town in America, that one seedy tavern that attracts winos, bums, and maybe... a serial killer.

The thunderous sound of "My Sharona" by the Knack told us the joint was rockin'. Judd and I took a deep breath and walked in.

We immediately felt out of place. Every eye telepathically communicated, *What are YOU doing at our party?*

As if on cue, "My Sharona" came to an untimely end. The driving bass line was replaced by the gruff voice of a man who looked like he'd been drinking since dawn.

"Who the hell are you guys?"

Judd and I looked at each other. One of the first things good journalists learn is how to talk themselves out of a sticky situation. Fortunately, we had both learned well.

"Oh, we just came by for a drink," I said with an innocent smile. "Hope that's okay."

"It's okay as long as you guys ain't reporters."

Technically, I was a producer, not a reporter. But I figured this was probably not a good time to argue semantics. "Well, to be honest, we do work in the media, but even journalists get thirsty now and then."

"Get this straight, dumbass. Your kind ain't welcome here," the drunk slurred. He leaned in closer to make himself clear. "You and your fucked-up friends are harassing our buddy, Angelo. If he's the Hillside Strangler, then I'm Jack the Ripper."

The drunken crowd behind him jeered in agreement. A lady shot us the finger. Even the bartender gave us the evil eye. With or without Judd, this was a bad idea. Time to plot our exit strategy. At that moment, I spotted a familiar face—

a face I'd only seen in photographs and on the news.

Angelo Buono.

We locked eyes for half a second through a blue haze of cigarette smoke. Then he got up and calmly strolled out the back door toward the parking lot. With all eyes on us, I suspect I was the only one to see him leave. I nudged Judd and nodded toward the door. He thought it was a signal for us to leave for safety's sake, but it was a whole lot more than that.

As we exited into the night, I whispered to Judd, "I just saw Buono come out here." Judd was smart enough not to react. He quickly absorbed the only two facts that mattered: One, Angelo Buono was close by; two, we better keep our cool.

We scanned the poorly lit parking lot. A few feet away, a couple was in a lovelock on the front seat of a beat-up Chevy. The sound of Vin Scully calling a Dodger game blared out of a nearby pickup truck. Then we spotted him. Buono stared at us from behind the wheel of his dark sedan.

Judd and I pretended we didn't see him and casually got into my car. I looked out the rearview mirror just in time to see our target take off.

"Should we follow him?" Judd asked.

I answered without hesitation, "Hell, yeah."

Buono pulled out of the parking lot then hung a right onto Colorado Boulevard. I tried to follow, but he had a good ten-second jump on me. Of course, we didn't have the legal authority to chase anyone—especially a convicted felon who could be armed and dangerous. And what would we do if we caught up to him? We weren't thinking straight. We knew he hated the media and we were a couple of young, unarmed journalists cruising late at night in an unfamiliar neighborhood.

When I hit the main drag, I was pretty sure he'd be gone. But there he was, stopped at a signal. I pulled up behind him.

"He's checking us out in his mirror," Judd said.

"Sure glad I'm not alone," I replied. "You know, all the research says he has a hell of a temper. Even if he's not involved in the stranglings, this guy's no saint. I heard he's a crazed sex maniac who gets off on humiliating women."

We stared in silence at the car in front of us. The hour was late, the road nearly empty.

"Let's play it by ear," I said. "See where he takes us."

Thoughts of Phil Spector's gun crept into my brain. Now I was tailing a possible serial killer. I wondered if I was pushing my luck. Judd must've been on the same drug I was, a lust for excitement and danger, because we stuck it out with Buono.

When the light changed, Buono drove through the intersection then hung a right onto a quiet residential street where most residents were likely sound asleep. He drove at a snail's pace. Several times, he appeared to stop but soon took off again. Since we were the only car behind him, no doubt he knew he was being followed.

Constantly checking his rearview mirror, Buono made another right, then a quick left onto a quintessential, tree-lined, middle-class-neighborhood street with ample sidewalks and white picket fences. Earlier in the day, it was probably packed with kids. But at this eerily quiet hour, the only ones awake were two up-and-coming journalists and a multiple-murder suspect. Stomach acid burned a hole in my gut.

Midway down the dark block, Buono pulled over. I stopped a mere fifteen yards behind him. Though I'd love to say it was out of bravery, stupidity would be more accurate.

"What the hell do we do now?" I asked Judd.

"Stay calm," he said, although his rattled voice told me he wasn't following his own advice. "If he approaches us, just say we want to interview him. He'll probably say no, and we'll call it a night."

Something told me it wouldn't be that simple. Only five minutes went by, but it felt like thirty. My heart beat as loud and hard as a hammer. My gut screamed at me to drive away, but what respectable journalist runs with his tail between his legs from what might be the interview of the year?

Then again, my bravery—a.k.a. stupidity—could leave me dead. While reviewing my options, directly ahead of us a car door creaked open. A leg stepped onto the asphalt, and a man with black, frizzy hair emerged. Angelo Buono was coming our way. Worse yet, he headed toward the driver's side of my car.

Angelo Buono was coming to see *me*.

The mustached figure prowled closer, like a pit bull with distemper. As he neared, I noticed gold chains around his neck, a gaudy turquoise ring on his large, knuckled hand, and those black, cold, *I-could-kill-you-if-I-want-to* eyes.

My engine was still running. With my hand on the stick shift, I was ready to pop the clutch and gun it down the street. When Buono was a few feet away but still advancing toward my car, he motioned for me to roll down my window. I could see both his hands. Neither held a weapon, so I opened the window. But just a crack.

"Why are you guys tailin' me?" he asked, his unshaven face about an inch from my window.

My brain momentarily froze, but I managed to respond, "We're hoping you wanted a chance to tell the media your side of the story."

"We don't mean you any harm," Judd said, leaning in Buono's direction. "We're just reporters trying to do our job. Do you want to do a brief interview?"

"About what?" Buono snapped back.

I sensed his agitation rising to nuclear level. Those icy eyes got even colder.

"You know, that so-called Hillside Strangler thing," I said, as if there was any doubt.

"Screw that Hillside Strangler crap." Buono's craggy face turned red with rage. "My cousin is the biggest liar on earth. I didn't kill nobody, and nobody can prove I did."

We hadn't even had a drink at the bar, but if we had, what Buono said next would've sobered us right away.

"Listen here, you two," Buono snarled, licking a glob of spittle from the corner of his mouth. "If I ever catch you following me again, you're gonna be sorry."

He reached inside his coat like he was reaching for a gun. "Now get the hell outta here," he growled. "I better not see your faces anymore."

Buono ended his pit-bull rant with a twisted grin and an ominous warning. "Got the message?"

We got the message. Judd and I sped away as fast as we could.

But we had one more thing to do before declaring safety. Judd's car was still parked by Buono's house. With lumps lodged high in our throats, we raced back to the house, hoping to get there before Buono did. Hunched down behind the steering wheel, I waited nervously in my car while Judd got into his. When he started his engine, we got the hell outta there, without the mad dog catching us.

In retrospect, I wasn't too disappointed I didn't get the interview with Buono that night. Instead, I was grateful I dodged another bullet.

It didn't take long for Buono's creepy world to collapse. Fibers found on victims Judy Miller and Lauren Wagner perfectly matched furniture in his house. Animal hairs found on Lauren's hands matched the rabbits he raised in his backyard. Detectives were able to piece together a claim by Bianchi early on that he and Buono would sometimes impersonate police officers in order to coerce their victims. When they discovered Buono's wallet held the telltale imprints of a police badge, police knew they had found Strangler #2. Evidence showed most of the women were brutalized and murdered at Buono's place then left on nearby hillsides in his familiar territory.

The burning question I and every other news reporter had was, *Why did the sociopathic cousins work together?* Police theorized neither one would have done it alone. But, together, they became a killing machine—two hotheaded losers convinced that women had done them wrong. Buono got a sick thrill by torturing them. Bianchi, by killing them.

But the uncoupling of this unholy pairing turned out to be their downfall. After moving north to Bellingham, Washington, Bianchi tried to "work" without his sidekick. Unfortunately for him, he lacked Buono's skill for cleaning up his tracks, and his solo efforts were soon exposed.

With more than ample evidence, both men were sentenced to life in prison without parole. Bianchi avoided the death penalty by testifying against his older cousin. Jurors inexplicably denied the prosecution's request that Buono be sentenced to the gas chamber. Instead, they felt the pair should receive the same sentence, even if it was less than they deserved. The judge was outraged by the decision but couldn't overturn it. Every reporter I knew felt the sentences were unjust. It's never easy to wish death upon another human being, but if anybody deserved to breathe poisonous gas, it was the Hillside Stranglers.

Eventually, Buono did have to answer to a higher authority. In 2002, he was found dead in his jail cell, supposedly of a heart attack. Some speculated that one of his cellmates or a guard decided to carry out what the justice system wouldn't. Bianchi, on the other hand, is living out his despicable life in a Washington penitentiary.

Sadly, my friend Judd Rose passed away of a brain tumor at the way-too-tender age of forty-five. Judd left behind a wife, two children, and a solid reputation as one of the finest journalists in the business. I have no doubt he's in a far different place than Angelo Buono.

As for me, the whole Strangler experience remained imprinted in my mind. It was the second time I'd run into a potentially life-threatening situation. First, Spector. Then, Buono. By all rights, the combination should have given me pause about where I was headed. My curious need for excitement and danger didn't exactly put me on the road to a long, healthy life.

But I didn't care. I lusted for my seductress. Common sense didn't stand a chance.

LOVE

Choose a job you love, and you will never have to work a day in your life.

–Confucius

CHAPTER 5
RUNNIN' DOWN A DREAM

Summer 1979

MARGARET THATCHER becomes the first female prime minister of the United Kingdom; the sports network ESPN premieres, proving there are actually people who want to watch Lithuanian rugby at 3 a.m.; and I'm livin' the dream.

# # #

My family, especially my father, was pleased—and, more likely, relieved—that the rambunctious kid who didn't seem to follow the rules had found his calling. Thanks to an exciting job, a flat stomach, and a full head of hair, I had no problem getting dates, which expanded my already inflated sense of self-worth even more. Looking back on it now, I was on a selfish high and can freely admit there were times I could have been a better person to those around me.

Even beyond my active social life, what I looked forward to most was going in to work every day. In fact, I would have done it for free. So, when I accepted a dream job offered to me by CBS Network News, seduction turned into love.

I couldn't believe, while still in my twenties, I now made my living at the home of *60 Minutes*, *Face the Nation*, and, in my opinion, the finest program on commercial television, *Sunday Morning*. Their flagship broadcast, *The CBS Evening News*, was the undisputed leader in both quality and ratings.

CBS Television City

I was assigned to the Western Bureau, where we covered everything west of the Rockies via CBS Television City in Los Angeles. The cavernous complex was a TV junkie's paradise. We shared the premises with shows like *All in the Family*, *The Carol Burnett Show*, and *The Price is Right*. These days, TV City is more likely to be associated with talent-competition shows like *Dancing with the Stars* and *America's Got Talent*. TV City was only about five miles from KNXT but was in a whole different world. It felt like I was going from community college to Harvard.

Talk about journalism history. Ever since they broke the story of the Lindberg kidnapping in 1932, CBS News gave the world a front-row seat to history like nobody else. After all, these were the folks who brought World War II into America's living rooms. Notable people who've worked at CBS News could fill the Broadcasting Hall of Fame: Edward R. Murrow, Mike Wallace, Diane Sawyer, Bill Moyers, Leslie Stahl, Charles Osgood, Bob Schieffer, Ed Bradley, Andy Rooney, Morley Safer, and, of course, "the most trusted man in America," Walter Cronkite.

At CBS Network about 1982

I felt both honored and humbled to work for the same company as these legends, as well as apprehensive. Oh, I might as well admit it: I was nervous as hell that I might be exposed as a fraud. How dare I pretend I was talented enough to work alongside the best in broadcasting? Even though I took a step down in title to get my foot in the door—weekend assignment editor and field producer— part of me was afraid they'd quickly discover I wasn't ready for the Major Leagues and send me back to the Minors.

While I did my best to appear strong and never let 'em

see me sweat, I'd do just about anything to keep my job:

Put in a sixty-hour week? *No problem.*

Work till midnight, be back in at eight? *Sure.*

Cover for a co-worker who was too hungover to come into work? *Absolutely.*

Most everyone kept a packed suitcase ready to go, since the nature of news is that anything can happen and it usually does. Extremes are the norm. One day, everything's blowing up. The next, everything's burning down.

CHAPTER 6
ALL SHOOK UP

IN MY LINE of work, you definitely need a love—or at least a tolerance—for the unexpected. Case in point: two life-changing events in 1980.

Mount Saint Helens Eruption
(Courtesy: National Oceanic and Atmospheric Administration)

When Mount Saint Helens blew her top, half the CBS News western bureau was suddenly dispatched to the Pacific Northwest, where some of us stayed for weeks. It turned out to be the most destructive volcanic eruption in United States history: fifty-seven people killed, ash scattered over eleven states, and countless landscapes changed...forever.

Harry R. Truman (Courtesy: U.S. Geological Survey)

Beyond the visual shock of Helen's outburst and resultant devastation, my most vivid memory is that of an eighty-three-year-old codger named Harry R. Truman (no relation to President Harry S. Truman). Ol' Harry and his sixteen cats ran the Mount Saint Helens Lodge near the base of the volcano. Even though scientists warned him the mountain was about to blow, Harry was having none of it.

He defiantly told reporters, "I've been here half a century. Ain't no way that mountain gonna hurt me."

Most of my fellow members of the media laughed at Harry and portrayed him as a stubborn ol' coot who probably belonged in the nuthouse. But I found him to be sharp-witted and likable. Harry said he owed his life to the fact that he'd refused to obey orders when his ship was torpedoed by the Germans in World War I. More than 200 of his fellow soldiers lost their lives. He never trusted authority after that. Later, when several family members died at an early age, Harry sank into depression until he found peace at the base of his beloved mountain, where he had remained for fifty-two years. After hearing his story, I gained a new respect for Harry and could see why he refused to pack up and leave.

Sadly, the scientists were right. Soon after he became a media star, Harry and his lodge were instantly buried under 150 feet of volcanic debris, never to be seen again. I took solace in the words of his friend: "Harry always said he wanted to die there, and he hoped it would be quick. He got what he wanted."

A few months later, I received another profound lesson in expecting the unexpected.

November 21, 1980

I pulled into my parking spot at TV City in an upbeat mood; it looked like an enjoyable Friday was on tap. Legendary CBS correspondent Charles Osgood and I were scheduled to drive out to Riverside to do a light feature story for the show *Sunday Morning*. Our interview subject had one of the most famous faces in American art, yet almost no one knew her name.

American Gothic by Grant Wood

Nan Wood Graham was the model used to create the somber woman in the classic painting *American Gothic,* by Grant Wood. Many people know it as the "pitchfork-couple painting": the stern farmer holding a pitchfork with a tight-lipped lady dressed in black by his side, both of them standing in front of their Gothic-style house.

Nan was Grant's sister and posed for the famed oil back in 1930. Now in her eighties, she had consented to a rare interview.

Ever since I first saw the painting as a child, it gave me the creeps. The dour look on the couple's faces was enough to turn milk sour. But I would never get to meet Ms. Graham. Just as Charlie and I hit the freeway, a frantic voice crackled from our car radio:

"Return to base! The MGM Grand is on fire!"

One of the largest hotels in the world stood engulfed in flames on the Las Vegas Strip—our feature story about the model for a famous painting would have to wait for another day. As we raced back to TV City, correspondent David Dow and his producer, Jim Anderson, were already en route to a waiting Lear jet at Van Nuys Airport. We all instinctively knew this was an all-hands-on-deck story.

Back at TV City, I dropped off Charlie, since hard-breaking news wasn't his area of expertise and he had to fly back to New York. Correspondent Terry Drinkwater, cameraman Bob Dunn, soundman Dick Johnson, and I raced to the airport, where CBS had arranged a second Lear to whisk us to Sin City.

As we listened to live radio reports on the way to the airport, the gravity of the situation became more and more evident.

"Two dead."

"Five dead."

"Ten dead."

We boarded the six-passenger jet and skyrocketed over the Mojave Desert toward Las Vegas. About the time we were over Barstow, we spotted smoke billowing thousands of feet in the air from the heart of the Strip.

"My God, this is huge," Terry said as he looked through one of the jet's windows. "There's tonight's lead story."

If anyone knew a lead story, it was Terry Drinkwater. He had covered nearly every major news event west of the Rockies for decades. Always in the thick of things, Terry stood a few feet away from Robert Kennedy the night he was assassinated. Dan Rather once described him as, "One of the people who helped invent television news reporting."

In addition to reporting stories, Terry anchored the West Coast editions of the CBS Evening News, covering events that occurred after the East Coast version with Walter Cronkite had aired.

"At least the smoke is starting to turn white," I said. I'd heard white clouds usually indicate a fire is under control; hopefully, that logic applied in this situation. Contrary to popular belief, most journalists aren't fans of mass tragedy.

But any optimism we held onto was quickly dashed by what we saw on our final approach to the Las Vegas airport. Sheets and blankets, waving like sorry flags from the top-floor windows of the twenty-six-story resort, told us that trapped hotel guests were desperately trying to get the attention of rescuers below.

Our driver, a courier from the local CBS station, KLAS, navigated three miles through heavy traffic and delivered us to the north side of the MGM Grand shortly after nine o'clock in the morning. By then, the fire was mostly under control, but the extent of the tragedy was just beginning to become evident.

Standing amidst a sea of firefighters, media, and stunned survivors, I did my best to process the surreal images in front of me: an elderly couple in a tearful embrace...a trembling teenaged girl sitting on a curb...a frustrated fireman who looked like he was on the verge of a heart attack. In all the stories I've covered before or since, I've never felt so much vulnerability in one place.

Thick air clogged my nostrils, leaving a pungent taste of soot while smoke scratched at my throat. Beyond the yellow *DO NOT CROSS* tape, powerful visuals continued to hit home: desperate looks on the faces of rescuers, even though the flames were out; firefighters' ladders that only reached a third of the way up the side of the hotel; sheets and blankets still hanging from windows, even though I couldn't see any faces peering out from behind them.

A sobering reality hid behind the walls of the charred building. Many of the people trapped inside the hotel wouldn't be taken to the hospital. They would be going to the morgue.

When the MGM Grand opened in 1973, the builders proudly proclaimed it the world's largest hotel. From its 2100 opulent rooms to its dozens of marble statues and a casino large enough to hold three football fields, the megaresort was a forty-three-acre ode to hedonism. Now, it was a burning, sacrificial temple of gloom.

The time came to put emotions aside and get to work. All of us went in search of interview subjects and B-roll— that's an old film term meaning the supplemental camera shots that are shown during an interview or voice-over. Meanwhile, our dedicated colleague, David Dow, took on two jobs. While putting together his story for that night's TV broadcast, he found time to sandwich in live radio reports.

David was the calming force in what was turning out to be one of the biggest stories of the year. Unlike many reporters I worked with in my career, I never saw him drink, swear, or even get angry. But even David found it hard to keep his cool when, a few feet away from him, a tragedy mercilessly unfolded.

Twenty-one dead.

Thirty-four dead.

Forty-eight dead.

Burning to death must be the worst possible way to go, I thought. But I soon learned that most of the victims never got anywhere near the flames. While they slept, a fire-breathing monster came to life many floors below. Frayed wires above the casino delicatessen set off sparks that went undetected for hours. Just after seven o'clock in the morning, a construction worker noticed a flickering light coming from the restaurant, even though it was technically closed for business at that early hour. Upon closer inspection, he spotted flames, called security, and hunted for a fire extinguisher.

He had no idea what he was up against.

Within minutes, a fireball burst through the ceiling and roared through the deli. Fueled by wallpaper, carpet, glue, and plastic, (a lawyer would later say, "The MGM was built in the golden era of plastics.") hungry flames took dead aim at the casino. Firefighters later estimated the inferno traveled at fifteen to nineteen feet per second, devouring slot machines, blackjack tables, and gamblers before it exploded out the main entrance along the Strip.

Despite the flames and chaos, many of the hotel's estimated five thousand guests were oblivious to the drama unfolding many floors below. Cincinnati Reds pitcher Tom Hume, who was on the twenty-fourth floor, later told a reporter he thought the commotion was coming from rowdy gamblers. He said to his wife, "Don't pay any attention to those people. This is Vegas. There's nothing to be alarmed about."

Tom, Mrs. Hume, and most everyone else in the hotel had no way of knowing that the thick, black, toxic fumes had only one place to go...up. No idea that the fire alarms would be strangely quiet. No clue that the hotel's faulty ventilation system would soon pump deadly carbon monoxide into the rooms of unsuspecting hotel patrons.

The pitcher and his wife survived, but many of their fellow guests did not. Numerous victims died of smoke inhalation in the stairwells when, after heading for the stairs, all the doors automatically locked behind them. The lucky ones were overcome in their sleep.

Fifty-two dead.

Sixty-seven dead.

Seventy-three dead.

Memory is selective, particularly when it's forged in tragedy. Much of that day is a blur; it plays back in scenes: Reverend Billy Graham, in town for three days of evangelism, comforting the dazed victims...a drunk holding what appeared to be a scorched casino chip...the chaos across the street at the Barbary Coast casino, where a lounge had been converted into a makeshift medical area.

Being busy can be a blessing, especially when you're surrounded by panic, frustration, and sadness. I did my best to help as Terry anchored the West Coast edition of the CBS Evening News from the north side of the MGM Grand, on Flamingo Road. I think he told me I did a great job, but I was in no mood to accept compliments. I just wish I could have done more to help the people inside the hotel.

When David reported the lengthy lead story about the fire for the TV broadcast, he included an exclusive, heartbreaking account of a woman frantically searching for her missing husband amidst utter chaos and tragedy. Fortunately, the couple later reunited, giving David at least *one* upbeat story to report during that horrendous day.

By the time we were packed and ready to leave, all of us were mentally and physically exhausted. On the plane ride home that night, we barely spoke a word. It wasn't long after that trip before residual feelings of sorrow turned to anger. When investigators later dissected the tragedy, they discovered a staggering *eighty-three* building code violations. They learned that, in addition to the faulty ventilation system, locked doors, and silent fire alarms, there were no sprinklers installed in the restaurant or even in much of the casino.

Despite pressure from fire marshals during the hotel's construction, MGM executives didn't want to fork out the extra money, so they convinced a building inspector that sprinklers weren't needed. Their reasoning? The restaurant and casino were open twenty-four hours a day. If something were to catch fire, *somebody* would always be present to quickly notice any flames. The building inspector didn't consider that, someday, the restaurant might change its hours of operation, which is exactly what happened by 1980. He didn't consider the need for sprinklers when *nobody* would be present to stop this fateful fire.

Ironically, the only area of the building that had inspired MGM executives to pull out their wallets and ensure utmost fire protection in an otherwise-hotbed hotel was not one open to the public, nor was it accessible to most employees. That precious outlay of money and protection was afforded to none other than...the money counting room.

A total of eighty-five people lost their lives on that horrific fall morning. Another 700 were injured, including guests, employees, and fourteen firefighters. The tragedy remains the worst disaster in Nevada history and the third-most deadly hotel fire in modern U.S. history. Incredibly, only one victim died of burns alone. Nearly all the rest succumbed to smoke inhalation and carbon monoxide poisoning.

But something positive emerged from the ruins of that tragic event. Nevada now has some of the toughest fire safety regulations in the country. Today, if a blaze erupts in a hotel on the Vegas Strip, you have a better chance of being drowned by overhead sprinklers than of being consumed by flames.

Whenever I think back to November 21, 1980, I envision those who suffered the tragedy of the MGM Grand fire—heck, I even visualize ol' Harry Truman, the lodge keeper who paid dearly for defying Mount Saint Helens—and remind myself that, indeed, life can change in a heartbeat.

That day, forever burned into my memory, often makes me ponder the question, *With moments left to live, what will be most important to me?*

CHAPTER 7

WHY DON'T YOU COME UP AND SEE ME SOMETIME?

LESS THAN TWENTY-FOUR hours after returning from covering the MGM fire, I received yet another unforgettable reminder that *anything* can happen in the news business. While still recovering emotionally from the death and destruction in Las Vegas, I found myself drudging through my workday. About halfway through my shift, I casually picked up the news hotline.

"CBS News. Davis."

"Listen to me. I've got something very important to tell you," a male voice said.

"Who is this?"

"Doesn't matter. CBS was her favorite network. Haven't called anyone else. I want you to be the first to know."

"Know what?"

"A legend has died."

"Who?"

"Mae West." *Click.*

You get used to crank calls in the news business, but something about this voice rang true. Sounded like an older guy, sincere, no BS.

If true, we had a major exclusive, the lead story on that

night's broadcast—only a couple of hours away. In those days, everybody knew Mae West. The queen of the sexual double entendre ruled the box office during the thirties and forties, and, in more recent decades, her movies had become a staple of late night TV.

Mae West

I knew I had to act on this information, but how? Caller I.D. hadn't been invented yet, so I had no clue who was on the other end of the phone. If I made calls to people who could verify the story, they might tip off the competition.

Then it hit me.

Several years before, a girl I was dating pointed out where Mae West lived: the penthouse of the elegant Ravenswood apartment building in the upscale Hancock Park district of L.A. Mae had called the Ravenswood her home for half a century. When the sex symbol of her day said, "Come up and see me sometime," the Art Deco masterpiece was where the lucky invitee would take her up on her offer.

I knew the neighborhood because my great-grandfather built hundreds of homes in the area. Since it was just down the road from TV City, a thought stirred in my head: *Why not drive a few miles over to Mae's place to see if she's still among the living?*

A co-worker agreed to cover for me.

I jogged through the halls of TV City, past the set of *The Young and the Restless,* and out to employee parking. I jumped into my car and headed east toward Hancock Park.

When I pulled up to the Ravenswood, excitement turned to doubt. Zero activity, not a car parked in front. Even if Mae West had died in a hospital, there'd be a friend, a relative, *somebody* at her home of fifty years.

I found a parking place in front and walked into the spacious lobby of the seven-floor building.

Looks well preserved for a place built during the Depression.

A massive chandelier lit the white walls, antique mirrors, and marble floor. The scent of fresh-cut roses filled the air.

"Can I help you?" a voice echoed from the concierge across the room.

"I'm from CBS News. I understand Mae West lives here."

"I can't comment on our residents, sir."

"Well, we had a report that Miss West has passed on. Can you at least confirm or deny that?"

The man chuckled. "I can tell you Miss West is quite alive. Trust me, I'd know if that weren't the case."

I thanked him and returned to my car. *Damn, I've been conned. That jerk on the phone fooled me, wasted my time.* Only in the news business can you get angry because someone's not dead.

Then the journalist in me kicked in: *Don't take the word of some dude who works in the lobby.* I circled the block, parked across the street, and plotted my next move.

I spotted a family of five headed toward the Ravenswood lobby. Earlier, I'd noticed an elevator out of the concierge's view.

Maybe I can sneak behind that family and slip into the elevator unnoticed.

The plan worked.

I knew West lived in the penthouse, so I hit the button for the top floor. When the elevator opened, I saw only one apartment with double doors. That had to be the place.

I knocked once.

Twice.

The door opened.

A tall, muscular, middle-aged man with tears in his eyes asked, "Who are you?"

"My name is Ken Davis. I'm with CBS News. Are you all right?"

"No."

"I'm so sorry. I'm here because…"

"Come in, come in."

I found myself relieved he'd interrupted me. I didn't have to ask a crying man if Mae West had died. At least, not yet.

The door opened to a white foyer decorated in Louis XIV and Mae. Photos, portraits, and posters of the legend were everywhere.

"I'm Paul. She was such a wonderful person—lived with her for twenty-six years. Love of my life."

"I understand," I said, feeling my own eyes tear up.

Paul gazed at a statuette of Mae in her prime. "You're a young guy, probably think of her as that old actress with the sexy walk or the funny lady in the W.C. Fields movies, but she was way ahead of her time."

"Tell me more, Paul." I knew the network news aired in just over an hour, but I didn't have the nerve to stop a man in grief.

He led me down a short hallway, and then paused by a photo of Mae with Sammy Davis, Jr.

"Bet you didn't know Mae fought for civil rights when Martin Luther King was still a toddler. Back in the thirties, the building manager here didn't like it when she invited a black friend for dinner, so she bought the whole damn complex. Fired the guy."

"Appreciate the information, Paul, but I really need to ask…"

He ignored me and continued down the hall to a framed newspaper advertisement for her 1927 play, *The Drag*.

"Those gay-rights people got nothin' on Mae. Long before they were born, she wrote and starred in a couple of plays that featured homosexuals. Cops raided the theater, but Mae refused to shut down the show. Went to jail for her beliefs."

"Paul, I'm facing a deadline—have to ask you a difficult question."

Without missing a beat, he pointed to a poster of Mae and W.C. Fields from the 1940 movie, *My Little Chickadee*. "And don't get me started on Mae's film career. Did you know she didn't make her first picture until she was thirty-eight? Two years later, she was the second highest paid person in the country. Only William Randolph Hearst made more.

"Nobody had heard of Cary Grant until Mae spotted him walking around the studio, put him in *She Done Him Wrong*. Picture was so successful, it saved Paramount from bankruptcy."

Maybe Paul gave me the mini-biography so a journalist would get his facts straight. Or perhaps it was a defense mechanism to avoid crying. Either way, I was in panic mode. I still hadn't confirmed if Mae West was dead or alive.

"Paul, we're gonna have to end this tour. I need to know for sure. Is Mae gone? I can't call my bosses in New York without some kind of proof."

Paul took a deep breath and looked me straight in the eyes. "Come with me."

He led me through the small living room toward a large white door. The atmosphere seemed to get warmer as we got closer. Paul knocked once on the door then slowly turned the gold handle. A blast of humid air hit me as I followed him in.

Just inside the dark room, an elderly man sat in an armchair, flickering candles barely lighting his crinkled face. Out of the corner of my eye, I could see a huge circular bed against the far wall. I figured the old guy might be Mae's doctor, who'd show me a death certificate, but he didn't say a word.

There appeared to be a lumpy sleeping bag on the bed, and something feathery was poking out the top.

Strands of platinum blonde hair.

I diverted my eyes for a second to make sure they weren't deceiving me. When I looked back, a chill shot up my spine.

A forehead glistened in the candlelight.

The sight swallowed me. Everything else disappeared. Just Mae and me, alone in the dark. Instinctively, I went into self-protection mode and took several steps back. I glanced at Paul. He slowly nodded, as if to say, "*Yes, that's Mae.*"

That was enough for me. I sure wasn't about to unzip that sleeping bag for a closer examination.

I wanted to say, "Get me the hell outta here," but, fortunately, my words took a more respectful route. "Paul, I'm sorry for your loss." Offering a handshake, I wrapped it up with a polite, "I really should be going."

"I understand. Let me show you out."

Paul led me back through the living room, past the mini-Mae museum and into the foyer, where I spotted a phone. The newscast was now only forty-five minutes away, and the network bosses in New York had no idea I was sitting on a major exclusive.

"Paul, hate to ask you, but can I use your phone?"

"Of course."

I called a co-worker so he could tip off the main news desk in New York and tell them to pull Mae's obituary. All the major networks have pre-packaged obits about aging famous figures for cases like this. Sometimes, that prep work is creepy. I once had to interview actor James Cagney under the pretense that we simply wanted to do a segment about his favorite movies when, in fact, he had no idea we were preparing a story for his final curtain call.

I bid Paul a quick farewell and bolted for the elevator. On the ride down, my heart kicked into overdrive. In the last few minutes, I'd snuck into a building, consoled a crying man, and—oh, yeah—seen a dead movie star. Just another day in the news business.

When I reached the lobby, I knew I had to put my emotions on hold and contact New York. These were the days before cell phones, and there wasn't enough time to drive back to the office. Even if the lobby had a pay phone, I didn't want to deal with the cocky concierge making my life even more difficult.

So I headed to a gas station up the street. *Please let it have an empty phone booth, and please let me have change in my pocket.* It did and I did.

By the time I called the CBS News hotline in New York, there was less than forty minutes to airtime. I told the show producer what I knew, and he confirmed Mae's death would be the lead story.

"And one more thing," the producer said. "We want you to do a live radio report in six minutes."

Gee, this should be no big deal. Other than what Paul told me, all I knew about Mae West was that she was a faded sex symbol, popular well before my time. Now, in a few minutes, I'd have to tell her life story to millions of listeners worldwide on the CBS Radio Network.

A researcher got on the phone, gave me some quick details about Mae's life: born to a prizefighter and his wife in 1893; starred on Broadway in her teens; banned from radio for a decade because of her sexual innuendos; and appeared in a dozen movies. To fill out the rest of her story, I scribbled down the anecdotes Paul told me and prepared to wing it.

Moments later, I gave my radio report from the cramped phone booth as a tattoo-covered guy resembling a prison escapee pumped gas a few feet away. It's all a blur now, but I must've done something right, because the big boys in New York were pleased.

My job done, all I had left to do was wait for the start of the evening news. I got back in my car, headed to CBS, and walked into the newsroom just as the broadcast began:

"This is the CBS Evening News with Bob Schieffer."

"Good evening. A Hollywood legend has died. CBS News has exclusively learned that actress Mae West passed away today at the age of eighty-seven..."

After the story aired, my blood pressure finally returned to normal. It had been an exhausting two days, starting with the MGM Grand fire and ending with my experience with Mae. In the business, we call it "news overload."

I later found out "Paul" was Paul Novak, a former Mr. California who'd been a muscleman in Mae's old Las Vegas stage show. He was three decades younger than Mae and never left her side.

But I still have questions when I reflect back on that surreal day:

What was with all that secrecy?

Who was the other man in Mae's bedroom?

Why did Paul call CBS before an ambulance or coroner could take away Mae's body?

I still don't understand why all the secrecy, but my theory is the other man was probably Mae's doctor, and Paul couldn't bear to see the love of his life taken away. As for Paul calling us, maybe he hoped he could gain closure by seeing the stark news of his beloved Mae on TV. Or, maybe, he simply wanted to give Mae the attention he felt she deserved.

I'll never know the answers to those questions. I wish I'd gone back and asked Paul, but I never did. Now it's too late. He passed away in 1999.

There was one more personal question that lingered with me after my visit to Mae's home. Why did the experience stick with me for years afterward? Sure, it was a shock to unexpectedly see her in that sleeping bag, but it was something more. Before her death, she was to me just an aging actress from another era. But afterwards? After putting myself in Paul's shoes, I had an enlightened view of Mae through the eyes of someone who truly loved her.

# # #

After my Mae West adventure, my stature at CBS continued to grow. In addition to field producing stories throughout the Western U.S., I did more live radio reports. And since the network news broadcast was three hours old by the time it aired in the West, I voiced occasional updates on TV. A full staff tended to these tasks during the week, but, on weekends, there were times when only a technician and I made that happen. It could get a little hairy—make that a *lot* hairy. I had to time my update to the second, since it had to be the exact length of whatever story it was replacing. Sometimes, being a good journalist requires being a good mathematician.

Soon, I was interviewing everyone from senators to sinners (occasionally, they are one and the same). But the most memorable conversation I had was with a fellow CBS employee.

CHAPTER 8
DON'T STOP BELIEVIN'

ONE OF MY FAVORITE things to do at CBS News was to answer the private hotline; you never knew who might be calling. Mike Wallace could be arranging an interview for *60 Minutes,* Leslie Stahl might be checking on a segment for the evening news, or, if I was lucky, it might be my favorite uncle. In fact, it seemed like he was *everybody's* favorite uncle.

The man had a neatly trimmed mustache, bushy eyebrows, and a plainspoken grace that made us trust his every word. He visited our living rooms every weeknight around dinnertime and was present for some of the most influential events of my generation's lives.

He celebrated with us when man first took steps where no human had ever walked before: "Whew! Oh boy. Armstrong is on the moon."

He took off his black-framed glasses and mourned with us when John F. Kennedy was assassinated. Many of us can still remember his exact words as he blinked back tears: "From Dallas, Texas, the flash, apparently official, President Kennedy died at one p.m., Central Standard Time."

And, contrary to popular belief, he introduced the Fab Four to America two full months before Ed Sullivan put them on TV: "In Great Britain, an epidemic called Beatlemania has seized the teenaged population."

He may have been just about every baby boomer's favorite uncle, but few can say they swapped stories with him over drinks and dinner. I was one of the lucky ones. Just like with Mae West, the adventure began with a phone call.

April 1981 – Los Angeles, CA

"CBS News Hotline. Davis."

"Hi. This is Walter Cronkite."

Walter Leland Cronkite. Not just another prominent journalist, but my journalism hero—the man poll after poll referred to as the most trusted man in America. When he signed off the news every night with, "And that's the way it is," we knew that's the way it was.

I did my best to treat him like a mere mortal. "Hi, Mr. Cronkite. How are you doing?"

"Doing great, thanks. I just finished covering the space shuttle landing, and I'm going to chopper in to the L.A. bureau. Can you set me up with a ride to the Beverly Hills Hotel?"

Cronkite was calling from Edwards Air Force Base, about ninety miles northeast of Los Angeles, where he'd been covering the space shuttle Columbia's return to Earth. He had stepped down from the CBS Evening News anchor desk a few weeks earlier, replaced by Dan Rather. It was only natural that his first story in semi-retirement was about his first love—space travel.

"No problem, Mr. Cronkite. What time do you think you'll arrive?"

"I'm guessing in about forty-five minutes. We'll call you when we're a few minutes out."

"Perfect. See you then."

The plan called for Cronkite to fly via helicopter to the roof of CBS Television City a.k.a. TV City. After Cronkite hung up, my first impulse was to call our news courier, Norman. It was his job to transport bigwigs when they came to town.

Then it hit me.

What am I thinking? I'm off in a few minutes, and one of my idols wants a ride to Beverly Hills.

I quickly wrapped up my work, giving myself just enough time to clean out my car. It's a safe bet an American icon didn't want to sit on a Willie Nelson tape and a half-empty water bottle.

I swung back by the newsroom, grabbed a walkie-talkie, and headed up to the roof to wait for Cronkite's helicopter. I got there early, not only because I was eager to meet the man, but because it was my favorite spot at TV City. On a clear day, you could gaze all the way from the majestic San Gabriel Mountains to the peaceful Pacific Ocean. There's nothing quite like a panoramic view of the City of Angels.

I plopped down next to the helicopter pad in a comfy, weather-beaten chair that was probably a soap opera castoff and radioed my co-worker at the assignment desk four floors below.

"Let me know when Cronkite calls with his E.T.A."

"Will do."

I drew in a deep breath of the chilly, late-afternoon air and thought about what lay ahead.

Would he be as pleasant in person as he seemed to be on TV? How did he feel about being replaced by Dan Rather? And perhaps most importantly, did he have dinner plans?

After a few minutes, my walkie-talkie crackled to life.

"Base to Ken. Cronkite called. He's approaching the city."

"Ten-four. Appreciate your help," I replied.

My nerves kicked in. I'd met presidents, movie stars, and homicidal maniacs. But this was Walter Cronkite, the prime minister of my profession.

Walter Cronkite (Courtesy: Arizona State University)

He anchored network television's first nightly half-hour news program and gave us a front-row seat to almost every major news event since World War II.

He had been awarded the Presidential Medal of Freedom (the highest honor a U.S. citizen can receive) and was on NASA's list to be the first journalist in space.

And he directly affected American policy by opposing the Vietnam War. When Cronkite came out against the war, President Johnson reportedly turned to his aides and said, "If I've lost Cronkite, I've lost middle America." Soon after that, Johnson decided not to run for re-election.

One of my goals when I first arrived at CBS was to meet the living legend. But since he was based in New York and

I was in L.A., the closest I'd gotten was about twenty feet away, at a stuffy network party. He was surrounded by high-level executives and low-level ass-kissers. Since I was neither, I'd kept my distance. Now, I would not only meet him, but his life would be in my hands as we navigated precarious Southern California traffic.

Soon, a black dot appeared in the silvery spring sky. As it neared, I could hear the clatter of the chopper's rotor blades beating the air into submission.

Whap-whap-whoosh. Whap-whap-whoosh.

The helicopter briefly hovered above me then slowly descended to a small, square landing pad.

I radioed the assignment desk. "The eagle has landed."

Cronkite's legendary smile sparkled through the rounded cockpit window. Moments later, the sixty-four-year-old emerged with extended hand. Gale-force winds from the rotors battered our faces and rearranged our hair.

"Hey there. What a beautiful day. Good to be back in Southern California."

"Hello, Mr. Cronkite. I'm Ken Davis."

"Well, Ken. Thanks for meeting me."

"Can I take one of your suitcases?"

"You betcha."

Cronkite and I left the rooftop with luggage in hand and stepped into the elevator, where we rode down to the first floor. I asked him if he wanted to swing by the news bureau to say hello.

"Nah, let's head out to the hotel," he answered. "I just want to get out of these dirty clothes. It was hotter than hell out there in the desert."

When the elevator opened at the ground floor, we stepped into the bustling CBS hallway shared by superstars and stage crew alike. Normally, no one batted an eye when they spotted a famous face. But this was Uncle Walter.

A nerdy-looking engineer who rarely spoke lit up when he saw him. "Hi, Mr. Cronkite. Welcome to California."

A sharply dressed young secretary nearly spilled her coffee. "I'm a big fan—I've watched you my whole life."

The master communicator made everyone he met feel like they were the most important person on the planet. I thought this is why America loves him. How weird it must be, though, to be recognized everywhere you go. The guy couldn't even walk down the street without being stared at.

Cronkite and I strolled out into the parking lot where I'd parked my car. Fortunately, I'd recently upgraded my wheels to a brand new, sporty Mazda RX-7.

Cronkite gave it a once-over. "Nice ride."

Walter likes my car. Thank God I paid extra for the deluxe interior.

I proudly unlocked the doors and helped load his luggage, then off we went. We exited the TV City parking lot and drove by some hippies who looked like they hadn't bathed since Jimmy Carter was president.

"Now I see why they call it Hollyweird," Cronkite joked.

"Yep. We attract all kinds here, Mr. Cronkite."

"Call me Walter," he said, as we headed up to Sunset Boulevard. "After all, we work for the same company."

"Sounds good to me. Walter it is."

It didn't matter that Cronkite—make that *Walter*—and I were on opposite ends of the CBS food chain. We got along like the best of buddies on our twenty-five-minute jaunt to the Beverly Hills Hotel.

"So, Ken, how are they treatin' you here in the bureau?"

"Can't complain, but we sure miss having you at the anchor desk."

Walter didn't respond. I couldn't understand why he'd stepped down when he was still the highest-rated anchorman on TV, but I didn't have the nerve to ask him... at least, not yet.

We hung a left onto the Sunset Strip. A young couple spotted my famous passenger, pointed, and waved at us from a VW on our right.

Walter smiled and mouthed through the window, "How ya doing?" They returned the greeting with enthusiastic thumbs up.

Moments later, Walter rocked my world almost as much as when he announced that man had landed on the moon. "I'm a fan of those guys," he said as we passed a massive Sunset Strip billboard for a popular musical group. Those guys were Pink Floyd. I'd have been more likely to believe that Liberace was straight than imagine Walter Cronkite was a fan of Pink Floyd. (Years later, he disclosed he also liked the Grateful Dead and even once appeared on stage with their drummer, Mickey Hart).

Even though he rarely visited Southern California, Walter knew it like a native.

"Hey, that's where Lana Turner was supposedly discovered," he said when we cruised by Schwab's Drugstore.

"Isn't that where the Doors got their start?" he asked as we passed the Whisky a Go Go. Nothing like having the most trusted man in America as your personal tour guide, even if it is in your own backyard.

Within minutes, the elegant Beverly Hills Hotel came into view. Known affectionately as the Pink Palace, it opened in 1912 before there was even a city called Beverly Hills. Entire books have been written about the place, but, in a nutshell, this is where: Gable and Lombard partied,

Tracy and Hepburn rendezvoused, and John and Yoko hid from the press. Liz Taylor spent six of her eight honeymoons there, Marilyn Monroe had her own table, and, to this day, it's a popular spot for Hollywood royalty to mix and mingle. You can see the Mediterranean-revival-style building on the cover of the Eagles album, *Hotel California*, as well as in movies like *The Way We Were* and *Beverly Hills Cop*. But if you want to stay at this living museum of Hollywood history, prepare to take out a second mortgage on your house.

We pulled into the hotel's long, palm-tree-lined driveway toward the entrance, where my new car suddenly didn't seem so special. But I couldn't have cared less. *To heck with you guys in your Ferraris and Lamborghinis. I've got Walter Cronkite riding shotgun.*

When I stopped the car, he casually asked, "Say, what are you doing for dinner, Ken?"

Before he finished saying my name, the answer jettisoned out of my mouth like a breaking news bulletin. "I'm a free man tonight, Walter."

"Tell ya what. Why don't you park the car while I go up to my room and get out of these dirty clothes? I'll meet you in the lobby in about twenty minutes."

"You got it."

I'm going to dine with Walter Cronkite. If only my old journalism professor could see me now.

Walter started to get out then paused. "Do you happen to know a place that's away from the public eye? I enjoy some privacy now and then."

"I know just the spot, Walter," I answered without thinking.

In fact, I had no clue. Nothing. Zero. Zilch. Finding a remote restaurant in Beverly Hills is like finding a secluded meadow on the Las Vegas Strip. But I opened my big mouth and lied to the most trusted man in America. I had twenty minutes to make good on my claim. Failure was not an option.

Walter went up to his room while I parked my car and strolled down a red carpet through the grand entrance of the hotel. The scent of fresh flowers and the sound of soft classical music did little to calm my nerves. I headed for a cushy, pale-pink chair under a chandelier the size of a Cadillac. Needed time to think.

Where can I take him? It's got to be away from the spotlight of Beverly Hills but close enough that we don't spend half the night driving.

Then it hit me. I'll call my ol' pal, Lindy.

For half a century, Lindy Brewerton tended bar at a Hollywood hole-in-the-wall called the Formosa Café. On the outside, it looks like a brick-red concrete box, but on the inside, it's a Cantonese cave of coolness. The former trolley car isn't on most tourist maps, so it was the perfect hangout for celebrities in need of privacy.

Remember the movie *L.A. Confidential*? The Formosa is where Lana Turner tosses her drink in the face of a stunned cop.

Over the years, Lindy served everyone from Bogie to Brando. He saw Frank Sinatra woo Ava Gardner, watched Lana Turner dance in the aisles, and observed gangster Mickey Cohen conduct "business." In more recent years, it's been a hideaway for the likes of Brad Pitt, Bono, Jodie Foster, and Johnny Depp.

I got to know Lindy when I worked around the corner at KCOP. My co-workers and I would sometimes drop by after the news. He had two desirable traits of every trusted bartender: he never forgot a name, and he knew how to give you your privacy. The Formosa seemed to be the perfect place for my "date" with Walter.

"Pardon me. Can you point me in the direction of a pay phone?" I asked the white-gloved concierge.

"Sir, it would be my pleasure to place a call for you."

You ever notice how, in luxury hotels, it's always the staff's "pleasure" to do something for you? I wondered if the concierge said that when his wife asked him to do chores at home.

"Why thank you. I'd like to reach the Formosa Café on Santa Monica Boulevard in Hollywood."

"Certainly, sir."

After dialing, he handed me the phone. "Hi, could I please speak with Lindy? Tell him it's Ken from Channel 13."

Moments later, a friendly, familiar voice came on. "Hey, Ken. How ya doing? Haven't seen you 'round here lately."

I explained the situation to Lindy, and he came through like I knew he would. He reserved us a private table.

I returned to my comfy chair and watched the passing parade of prosperity.

Isn't that what's-his-name from that Woody Allen movie...?

Hmmm, an old geezer with a young babe—wonder if she's his trophy wife...?

The daydreams came to an abrupt halt when Walter bounded out the elevator wearing a fresh set of clothes and a broad smile. "I'm hungry. Let's do it." With a light-colored blazer over an open polo shirt, he looked more like an excited game show host than the dignified gentleman who'd presented the news to thirty million people a night. We got back in my car to begin our twenty-minute journey.

"So, where we headed?"

"Ever heard of the Formosa Café?"

"Sounds familiar. Tell me about it."

Luckily, over the years, Lindy had filled me in on enough of the restaurant's famous past that I easily claimed my turn as tour guide for the night. "It's a hunk of Hollywood history. Opened back in the twenties to feed the stars at the nearby silent movie studios. Used to be just an old trolley car, but they later added a dining room and bar. It's not fancy, but it's where the famous go to get away from it all. Everybody from Bugsy Siegel to Marilyn Monroe used to hide out there."

Walter said the words I wanted to hear. "If it was good enough for Bugsy, it's good enough for me."

After several minutes of early evening traffic, we pulled into the Formosa's parking lot. It looked like it hadn't been paved since Bugsy was there and had since become a breeding ground for third-rate graffiti artists. I felt a knot in my stomach, like I'd ingested a bowling ball.

What was I thinking? You don't bring the most trusted man in America to a dive like this.

Fortunately, I was about to find out that the former Boy Scout from Missouri enjoyed being treated like a regular guy. After triple checking my car doors were locked, we made our way through the Formosa's shadowy back entrance. We were lured by hushed conversation, cigarette smoke, and a darkness that seemed to beckon: *Come in. I will hide you here.*

Walter loved it.

"This place is right out of a Raymond Chandler paperback," he quipped while scrutinizing hundreds of signed vintage photos lining walls and rafters. "There's Judy Garland, John Wayne, even Elvis. Perfect." The bowling ball in my stomach disappeared.

A debonair older man behind the bar placed an olive in a martini and looked up. "Ken, how nice to see you again. I have a special table reserved in the back room." Good ol' Lindy. He obviously recognized my dining partner but was far too classy to mention it.

"Great to see you, Lindy. You haven't changed a bit." I wasn't just being nice. The barkeep personified old school long before the term became popular, yet, somehow, he hadn't aged.

Lindy motioned to a nearby waitress. "Mary, the corner table in the back."

Our waitress, Mary Kay Moore, was a relative newcomer to the Formosa. She'd only worked there since Truman was president.

"This way, gentlemen," Mary said as she guided us past a dozen or so customers seated in aging red-leather booths. A few looked up, but no one seemed impressed to see America's favorite anchorman. Or maybe they didn't recognize him without his tie and newsman demeanor. Walter avoided eye contact with the patrons in the half-empty restaurant, determined to remain anonymous.

Mary led us into the original trolley car in the back. "Lindy said you wanted your privacy, so I won't seat anybody else back here unless the place gets packed. Can I start you off with a drink?"

Walter looked pleased. "Scotch sounds good to me."

In those years, I rarely drank hard liquor, but sharing a Scotch with a legendary journalist seemed appropriate. "Make it two."

Now that we were finally sitting face-to-face, three of his traits stood out: his twinkling eyes, his long fingers, and man, were those eyebrows bushy. While I studied his features, Cronkite checked out the Depression-era decor.

"This place is as old as I am."

"Well, I must admit, it's not exactly the Beverly Hills Hotel."

"Hey, this is a heck of a lot more interesting than the Polo Lounge," Walter said, referring to the fabled watering hole at his hotel. "People go there to be a celebrity. They come here to be themselves."

Soon after, Mary brought us our drinks and we ordered an appetizer. Walter got right to business. "So, what do you think of the new guy in the chair?"

I knew whom he meant but felt I had to clarify anyway. "You're referring to Dan Rather?"

"Yeah. What's the word on the street?"

Holy crap! Walter Cronkite is asking me, a rookie West Coast assignment editor, what I think of his replacement.

I couldn't decide if I should be a company man or say how I really felt. I went with the latter. "He's not half the anchorman you are, Walter. Why'd you step down?"

Walter took a sip of his drink and locked eyes with me across the booth. "First of all, Dan's doing the best he can, and there's a lot of pressure on him. But I must admit I miss it a lot more than I thought I would."

Walter's candor screamed for a follow-up question. No one I knew was aware of the real reason Walter had retired, or at least they weren't talking. I was about to practice my interviewing skills on the nation's premiere journalist when Mary set down a plate of spring rolls, and the conversation turned to what we wanted for dinner. I made a mental note to return to the touchy topic.

After we placed our order, the subject turned to the most boring man at the table. "Ken, tell me a little bit about yourself."

I felt like a Little Leaguer talking to Babe Ruth, so I kept it short. "Well, I started in broadcasting as a disc jockey in Arizona. Then I decided journalism was my calling, so I became a TV news anchor and reporter for a bit. Guess I wasn't pretty enough, so I went behind the scenes as a writer, producer, and assignment editor. Glad I took that route, 'cause it brought me to the best news organization in the world."

The old newspaperman let out a deep breath and tapped those long fingers on the table. "Well, you'll never be the best in this business unless you're willing to give it your all." He downed his drink and cleared his throat. "But that's not enough. You can't just pretend to be an objective journalist. You have to walk the walk."

Then he said something that I've repeated to journalism students over the years. "Respect your audience. A reporter's only job is to hold up a clear mirror and truthfully show what happened." He leaned closer. "Opinions have no place in our business. Even my kids don't know how I vote."

Walter signaled for more spring rolls while I remained silent. The man was in a groove and I wasn't about to stop him.

He continued, "The times, they are a-changing and not for the better. Part of the blame falls on one of the best programs on television, *60 Minutes*. That show proved you can make big money with broadcast journalism. Stations all over the country started seeing news as a profit maker, not as a public responsibility." He took another sip of his drink. "Too many news organizations only care about 'will it sell' instead of 'is it accurate?'"

Like an untimely TV commercial hijacking a dramatic scene, Mary arrived with our dinner. I was still reeling from the master's words and had barely touched my spring rolls, so more food was the last thing on my mind. With a couple of Scotches in him, Walter loosened up and shared with me a story about what is surely an anchorman's worst nightmare: a bout of diarrhea he had endured during a live newscast. There's nothing quite like discussing bodily functions over chicken and dumplings with Walter Cronkite.

I opted to continue with the theme as I revisited my earlier query. "Speaking of the throne, any chance you'll reclaim yours at the anchor desk?"

Walter chuckled. "No, I'm afraid this old sailor has left the port. Couldn't go back now if I wanted."

"So why'd you quit at the top of your game?"

Walter paused. "I told CBS I planned to step down in the next year or so, but I wanted to take my time. Even though their standard retirement age is sixty-five, I was confident they'd let me stay as long as I wanted. But the front office had other ideas."

"So they forced you out?" I was startled by the blunt words that shot from my lips. It's a safe bet that alcohol played a role in my assertive outburst.

"No, I wouldn't say that," the baritone said in a soft voice. "ABC started flirting with Rather, and CBS was afraid he'd jump ship. They asked me to let him take the reins early, and I agreed."

Walter's words said one thing, his demeanor another. He shrugged his shoulders and pulled at the corner of his mustache. It seemed he might be grappling with whether or not he had made the right decision. It couldn't have been easy for an admitted adrenaline junkie to suddenly quit after being up against a journalism deadline since he was sixteen.

"Do you miss it?"

Walter locked eyes with me. "You betcha."

I felt humbled and honored that this American icon trusted me—someone he'd only known a few hours—with such candid feelings. I had three thoughts on why he might do so. One possibility was he might have been tired after a long day and had too many Scotches to care. Or maybe he was using me to get the word out that he deserved better treatment by the network he'd helped lead to the top. The final possibility, the one that felt most right, was that Uncle Walter could very well be every bit the real person he always appeared to be on TV, trusting and trustworthy, just as I'd always imagined.

Years later, Walter would accuse Dan Rather of *playing* the role of a newsman instead of *being* one. I could see how that would bother Walter. He was the real deal.

The rest of our dinner is pretty much a blur, but the most important parts of our conversation were already inscribed on my soul. Cronkite's inspiring words removed any doubt I'd had about continuing on in broadcast journalism. I was convinced, more than ever, that it was what I wanted to do.

After Walter graciously picked up the tab, we headed for the door. But first, he insisted on going by the bar to thank Lindy. A glassy-eyed blonde who appeared to be drinking her dinner surveyed my six-foot-tall companion. "Hey, aren't you...?"

Before she could verbalize her thought, Walter interrupted her with his standard, friendly reply, "Hi there. Pleasure to meet you."

We got back in my car where the reinvigorated newsman in me switched on all-news radio, but Walter seemed disinterested. As we headed back to his hotel, it still felt like I was riding with an old buddy, even though our time together was only about as long as a newscast and a couple of sitcoms.

"So, you got a lady in your life, Ken?"

"Yep. I'm seeing a girl who's a reporter in Phoenix. But it's nothing serious yet."

Walter turned to me and shared two pieces of wisdom that have stuck with me ever since. I didn't know it at the time, but they changed my life.

"Ken, you need a solid partner who will stick with you through thick and thin. Any success I've had, I owe to my wife, Betsy."

He let that marinate for a moment, then continued. "And, if you ever do get married, you might consider someone who doesn't make their living in our crazy business. I've found that one inflated ego in the house is more than enough."

Too soon, we were back on the stately streets of Beverly Hills, where a familiar, dignified structure protruded above the palm trees ahead of us. Under the cloak of darkness, the Pink Palace stood ready to welcome back American royalty. When we arrived at the entrance, Walter extended to me the same hand that has touched everyone from world leaders to everyday folks.

"Ken, I had a wonderful time. All the best to you and your career."

"Walter, it's been a night I'll never forget."

# # #

The next few days, I couldn't stop thinking about my heart-to-heart with Uncle Walter. Of all the subjects we discussed—his candid talk about the broadcasting business and the reasons for retirement—what stuck in my soul was what he'd said in the end about the importance of having a significant other to accompany me on my journey through life.

Having come of age at the height of sex, drugs, and rock and roll, I dated my share of women in my twenties—blondes, brunettes, and a psychotic redhead who was crazy enough to make Phil Spector seem sane, especially when she tried to tell me, "Charles Manson is simply misunderstood."

Over the years, though, I became close with some wonderful women who were definitely marriage material, but I was still too caught up in myself, my job, or both to take those relationships any further.

I began to think Uncle Walter was right; maybe I did need a solid partner at my side. It's a cliché to say that behind every great man is a great woman, but clichés exist for a reason—they're often true.

I thought about my parents, my sister Ellen, my close buddy Darryl Meathe, whom I've known since we were in preschool. All happily hitched for years and better for it. Maybe the time had come to take this marriage thing seriously. Following Walter's advice, all I had to do was find someone who didn't make her living in show business.

Enter a young lady from Denmark who knew as much about the TV biz as I did about Scandinavian horticulture. She had barely heard of Walter Cronkite and thought an anchorman was the guy who kept a boat from drifting away. What I admired right away, though, was that she could spot a phony person across a crowded room while blindfolded.

We clicked right away.

Jette (pronounced "Yett-eh") was in Southern California working for the Danish Consulate, and had only been here a couple of months when we met. We quickly learned a lot from each other. She introduced me to European customs and sensibilities that proved refreshing to a guy who grew up in the cradle of capitalism. She kept my priorities in order and taught me to not take my career or myself so seriously. I enjoyed showing her my beautiful country and the advantages of a big city, something that contrasted sharply with tiny Denmark.

Together, we shared a common love of animals, soul music, and offbeat humor, not to mention a common belief that she should stay on the American side of the Atlantic. Despite her mistrust of Hollywood types, it didn't take long for Jette to savor the fruits of the entertainment capital of the world. She enjoyed the backstage passes, upscale dinners, and occasional encounters with the rich and famous.

Within a few months, she moved into my Altadena home.

Afterwards, two questions remained for the powers that be to answer. Would Jette have the staying power to tolerate my love for and devotion to my demanding seductress, broadcasting? And would my seductress, so accustomed to my undivided attention all these years, tolerate my newfound desire for a thriving, steady private life with Jette? More than anything, I wanted all three of us to get along.

CHAPTER 9
YOU OUGHTA BE IN PICTURES

LIKE UNCLE WALTER said, TV people tend to have inflated egos, and I was no exception. It's a hell of a rush to decide who and what will be seen by millions of fellow earthlings. But the tables were turned in early 1982 when a colleague mentioned that one of the studios was holding what's known in Hollywood as a "cattle call."

"Hey, Ken, I hear Warner Brothers is auditioning news people for a movie. Wanna go and tryout with me?"

"Do I get to keep my clothes on?"

"Of course—it's not a horror movie!" He laughed. "All I know is it's about a TV reporter, nuclear weapons, and the CIA. It's got a slew of stars like Sean Connery and Katherine Ross."

Katherine Ross? *Oh, man.* That got my attention. I had a weak spot for the gorgeous actress ever since I first saw her in *The Graduate,* then later in *Butch Cassidy and the Sundance Kid.* When those movies played at Pasadena's Crown Theater, I saw them so many times I think the cashiers knew me by name.

And Sean Connery? Who would turn down a chance to work with the original 007? My buddies and I rushed to see every James Bond movie as soon as it was released. As far as we were concerned, Sean Connery was the *only* 007. All the other guys who played him later on were nothing but cheap imposters.

"Count me in," I said.

Bright and early the next Saturday morning, we showed up at Burbank Studios, where we encountered about twenty fellow broadcasters—all equally excited about the chance to be in a possible blockbuster.

Who knows? If I make the cut, maybe I'll get to be Katherine Ross's love interest.

Sure, my thoughts were delusional, but I had convinced myself anything can happen in showbiz.

We were directed to an enormous soundstage that looked like it could house a 747 with room to spare. In fact, a plaque on the front of the building stated the stage was so big, they'd used it to film the drag race in *Rebel Without a Cause*, the ballroom scenes in *My Fair Lady*, and had transformed it into an entire park for *The Music Man*. (Later, it became Gotham City for the *Batman* movies, an ocean for *The Perfect Storm*, a jungle for *Jurassic Park*, and, more recently, it made a brief appearance in *La La Land*.)

As we stood in awe of the 100-foot-tall house of dreams, a short guy in a purple sport coat approached us.

"Hi. I'm Hank, the director's assistant. Welcome to Stage 16—the tallest soundstage in North America." It was hard to take Hank seriously since he had the hair of a late-night televangelist and dressed like a color-blind used-car salesman. But I did my best to keep a straight face, figuring he was my ticket to scoring a speaking role.

"Our movie is titled *Wrong is Right*." Hank paused for effect and continued, "The story involves a globe-trotting TV reporter, nuclear weapons, and the CIA. We're looking for about eight broadcast news people—some of you will be chosen to be background players and at least one of you may get a speaking role. The director and our casting people will watch you from behind a glass booth."

"*Who's the director?*" yelled someone with typical newsperson chutzpah.

"Richard Brooks. You may have heard of him. He directed well-known movies like *In Cold Blood, Cat on a Hot Tin Roof, Elmer Gantry,* and *Looking for Mr. Goodbar.*" I couldn't picture the guy, but he had an impressive résumé. Those films had won a lot of Oscars. Some of them had come out when gasoline cost less than a buck a gallon, so I knew to expect he was up there in age. Or, as they say... seasoned.

"So, tell us about the flick," shouted a reporter from Channel 7. I chuckled. As if this guy was gonna turn down a chance to be in a major Hollywood film 'cause he doesn't like the subject matter.

Hank stared straight ahead and continued, "I'm not allowed to say anything about the story except that Sean Connery plays the TV reporter and some of you will play his co-workers. I can also tell you that some of the other stars include Katherine Ross, Leslie Nielsen, Robert Conrad, John Saxon, and a wonderful new actress named Jennifer Jason Leigh."

With that, we were led into the main section of the nine-story sound stage (where six stories are above ground and three are below). An intense blast of frigid air suddenly engulfed us from head to toe.

This movie better be a hit. How else are they going to pay for all this air conditioning?

A fictional newsroom and a television control booth took up one end of the stage. Above it all, a banner read *World Television Network.* The other end of the room gave us more clues about the movie's storyline. Full-sized set replicas of the Oval Office and the inside of CIA headquarters, surrounded by American flags and photos of dignitaries, filled that end of the room.

In an instant, twenty talkative news people were struck mute by the visual fusion of show business with political intrigue and journalism.

"I need each of you to go sit at a desk in our newsroom," Hank said. "I really don't care what you do. Talk on the phone...read the paper...whatever. Just pretend it's a slow news day and do what comes naturally."

So that's it? Just sit around and look pretty? How the heck am I going to stand out and get a role in this movie?

Moments after I found an empty desk, a deep voice boomed through a loud speaker: "Attention, everyone. The White House is under attack by terrorists!"

Some of the broadcasters looked surprised. Others, perplexed. A few of us quickly figured out the game. They want to see how we react to a major breaking news story.

For some reason, my inner Al Pacino kicked in. Maybe it was the espresso I'd downed on my way to the audition or the result of my new workout routine at the gym. In any case, I sprung to my feet and started barking orders. "Cutler, grab a camera crew and head to the White House! Rudzik, we'll have a helicopter waiting for you at the airport!"

To tell the truth, I don't remember what I said, but it was enough to get me the only significant speaking role awarded to our group. I felt bad that my buddy who'd told me about the audition was relegated to the background. To lessen the sting, I promised to buy him dinner after we wrapped.

To my surprise, they wanted to film my scenes later that

day. The upside of that was that it didn't leave me time to get nervous. Even though I had high hopes for sharing the screen with Katherine Ross, it wasn't meant to be. Early in the film, her character gets blown to smithereens by a terrorist explosion. Yes, showbiz can be brutal.

The full script was kept secret, but I did manage to gain a few insights about *Wrong is Right*. It was a combination thriller/black comedy involving nuclear weapons, the media, and various political nut jobs. Sean Connery would play a famous TV reporter who travels the world, hobnobbing with crazed Arab terrorists. I was to play "Ed," a control-room engineer who keeps Connery's character in touch with his TV news boss.

The script indicated I would briefly be on screen with 007 himself. Well... sort of. Sean's character would talk to me via satellite. My primary interaction would be with the actor Robert Webber, who had worked with everyone from Barbra Streisand to Paul Newman to Elizabeth Taylor. He played a general in *The Dirty Dozen*, a colonel in *Private Benjamin*, and juror number twelve in *Twelve Angry Men*. Now, he was slated to perform with a guy who hadn't acted since he was in backyard plays directed by his dad.

My character had three scenes in *Wrong is Right*. Fortunately, the shortest one would be shot first. Good for me—better to start out easy and get in the groove. For this scene, I only had to say five words: "On the audio satellite circuit." I'd never heard that phrase uttered in a newsroom or anywhere else but decided I was in no position to edit the script.

After a touch-up from the makeup lady, I took my seat at a workstation filled with flashing lights, teletype machines, and various high-tech gizmos to make me look like an engineering whiz. I repeated the five words to myself, again and again.

On the audio satellite circuit.

On the audio satellite circuit.

On the audio satellite circuit.

Sounds simple, but when several dozen people, three cameras, and the ghosts of historic Stage 16 are watching your every move, the pressure is on. Just as I was getting sick of hearing myself repeat that tongue twister, a stern-faced man who looked to be about seventy years old appeared from behind a camera.

"Hello, I'm Richard Brooks."

This was my first contact with the Oscar-winning director. His determined demeanor told me to shut up and listen.

"In this scene, Patrick Hale—Sean Connery's character—has just been in a horrible accident in the Sahara Desert. You don't know if he's dead or alive. The vice president of the network desperately wants you to find out his condition. Any questions?"

"No questions."

"Good. Let's do it."

Suddenly, a huge bank of lights glared down on me. They felt at least three times hotter than the ones we used on a TV set.

So this is why they keep this place so freakin' cold.

Three cameras moved in closer, followed by a loud shrieking bell that shook the wax in my ear canals. The entire building became eerily quiet. Out of nowhere, a young man jumped in front of my face and snapped a loud clapboard inches from my nose.

"Scene 5, Take One."

"Wait a minute!" Brooks shouted. "Put a pair of headphones on him."

Once that was accomplished, clapper-boy took another swipe at my nose.

"Scene 5, Take Two."

On the monitor, we see that, while reporting live from Africa, Patrick Hale's vehicle has overturned. Robert Webber's character bursts through the door and rushes up to me:

> WEBBER: *"Did you get through?"*
>
> ME: *"On the audio satellite circuit."*

Nailed it. Okay, it was only a quick line, but I delivered it like a matinee idol. My confidence soared.

After a few perfect backup takes, it was time for my second scene. This one was a bit trickier. It's later in the movie, when suicide terrorists are attacking Washington, D.C.

Robert Webber and I are watching Sean Connery's character report from the scene just as a helicopter explodes above the White House:

> CONNERY: *"Insane."*
>
> WEBBER: *"Put me through to Mr. Hale."*
>
> ME: *"He has a call, overseas—Hagreb."* (Hagreb— a fictional Arab country)
>
> WEBBER: *"Not now."*
>
> ME: *(angrily)* *"He says personal, urgent, and now!"*

Man, it feels good to talk back to the boss. This acting stuff is fun. Now my confidence bordered on cocky. I even asked a production assistant to grab me lunch as preparations were made for my last big scene. Being a "star" has its privileges.

My final on-camera appearance called for fewer lines but more, shall we say, thespian skills. Plus, I'd get to directly play off of Sean (at this point, I liked to think we were on a first-name basis, even if he surely forgot me soon after we met).

It's near the end of the movie, when a terrorist named Rafeeq threatens to blow up New York City unless the President of the United States resigns and is charged with murder. I've secretly recorded the threats.

SEAN: *"Ed?"*

ME: *"Yes, sir."*

SEAN: *"Did you tape Refeeq's call?"*

ME: *"Yes, sir."*

SEAN: *"Give it to the FBI."*

The script called for me to look nervous then hand over the tape to two intimidating FBI agents who are hovering over me. But first, I had to turn off the recorder and stop the spinning tape with my hand.

Take One: The recorder wouldn't turn off.

Take Two: The tape spun out of my hand and onto the floor.

I better stop screwing up. They can't cut me out of the movie, can they? Nah, I'm in too many scenes. Yeah, but still… Oh, c'mon, get it together, Davis!

Take Three: Score.

"Perfect," Brooks said. "That's a wrap."

I let out a sigh of relief.

Afterwards, I washed off my makeup, said my goodbyes, and headed out the door of Stage 16, feeling satisfied and a bit amazed at what I'd accomplished.

Only in Tinsel Town can you begin your day fighting

Southern California traffic, and end it dealing with terrorists and the FBI on a movie set. Though I didn't get to steal Katherine Ross's heart, I did get to hang out with 007 and soak in some serious Hollywood history.

Scene from Wrong is Right, *where I'm confronted by the FBI*
(Courtesy: Columbia Pictures)

Next came the tough part—waiting six months for the movie to be released. At first, my ego sought creative ways to share the news at every opportunity.

"Watcha been up to, Ken?" I imagined someone might ask.

"Oh, just waiting for my movie to come out this summer," I'd coyly reply.

"You're in a movie? That's awesome." Gush, swoon, etc.

Jette even told her relatives in Denmark they'd soon be able to see her American boyfriend on a sixty-foot-wide screen.

But as the premiere got closer, I became more and more anxious. Suppose they cut my scenes? What if I come across like an idiot? Am I going to regret this whole experience?

That's when I realized that most of the people I put in

front of a camera in TV news stories have similar fears. In the past, I'd looked at them as just another face to advance the story I needed to tell. But now, I knew what it was like to have my reputation on the line for something that was out of my control.

Finally, *Wrong is Right* opened in theaters. Jette and I were invited to Westwood to see it alongside bit players and members of the crew. For some reason, we weren't asked to attend the red-carpet premiere the night before. Obviously, whoever sent out the invitations didn't realize I was Sean Connery's "sidekick."

When the lights went down, I took a deep breath and settled into my seat. Two hours later, as the credits rolled, I had mixed emotions.

On the positive side, all of my scenes made the final cut and, in my biased opinion, I did pretty darn well, at least for an amateur.

On the negative side, although there was witty dialogue and superb cinematography, the story was convoluted and the middle portion of the movie was about as exciting as a TV test pattern.

Critic Rex Reed of the *New York Daily News* called *Wrong is Right* "a film of enormous brilliance, humor, imagination, originality, and style." Vincent Canby of the *New York Times* saw things differently and described it as "supercharged and uniformly silly." The public—the only critics who matter—essentially gave it a thumbs down. *Wrong is Right* didn't last long in theaters.

But at least the film holds a special place in movie history. It's uncanny how accurately it predicted what would happen in the coming decades. Islamic terrorists trying to topple the World Trade Center towers. Suicide bombers intent on destroying democracy. A war in the

Middle East fueled by politicians falsely claiming the enemy was hiding weapons of mass destruction. Fiction became truth in this case. Predictions about everything going so wrong in the world...were right.

CHAPTER 10

WHAT A WONDERFUL WORLD

ABOUT THE TIME *Wrong is Right* ended its run in theaters, an executive at PBS who knew I had once been a TV anchorman and reporter gave me a call.

"Ken, ever heard of the TV show, *Why in the World?*"

"Why in the what?"

"It's a national, weekly program where high school students question experts about a different topic each week, running the gamut from religion to rock and roll. Our regular guy is going on vacation, and we'd like you to host a couple of shows."

"Why me?"

"Well, the program is aimed at young people, and, frankly, our regular host could be their grandfather. Not to mention, he's got an ego the size of Alaska. We need a young, fresh face, so I thought of you. How 'bout I send you a tape, so you can check it out?"

I felt honored—no, make that thrilled—to be asked. In fact, I immediately knew I wanted to do it. But, in the broadcasting business, too much excitement about a job prospect can be seen as a sign of weakness, so I answered in my best nonchalant voice, "I'll let you know after I run it by the suits at CBS."

Once my bosses gave me the go-ahead, I had to move quickly, since the shows aired within a couple of weeks. Fortunately, the format was simple. The first part of the program was a pre-taped segment with several experts whom I'd interview in their homes about that week's topic. The remainder of the show revolved around the students questioning one of the experts in the studio.

The studio part was easy. All I had to do was moderate the discussion and act like I had a few working brain cells. I figured it should only take a few hours to shoot. The pre-taped segments out in the field were a whole other story. For those, I had to go on location, interview the expert, write my narration, and work with an editor to turn the pretty pictures into a snappy segment. That takes time— something in short supply.

The first show focused on the fascinating world of architecture and the significant role it's played throughout history. Guests included esteemed architects such as Tim Vreeland, Peter Kamnitzer, and the legendary John Lautner, who held the distinction of having worked closely with Frank Lloyd Wright and was the official architect for the 1984 Olympic Games. The subject matter was not my area of expertise, but the show went well.

The theme of my second episode of *Why in the World?* was a topic I was much more familiar with: creativity in the entertainment world. For this show, the plan called for sound bites from luminaries like actor Martin Sheen, musician Herbie Hancock, composer Aaron Copland, TV personality Steve Allen, and dancer Juliet Prowse, followed by the main guest being interviewed by the students.

"We booked a guy who can talk about everything from Shakespeare to Broadway," the show's producer said with the confidence of a winning politician on election night. "What do you think about Charlton Heston?"

Charlton Heston? Are you kidding me? The students won't be able to relate to him.

Sure, he'd had his day in the spotlight when he starred in movies like *Ben Hur*, *The Ten Commandments*, and *Planet of the Apes.* But most of that had happened before many of these kids were even born.

I told the producer that Heston was not the best choice for our main guest and should be replaced. (Guess I was feeling a little full of myself, following my stint at "movie stardom.") PBS agreed, as long as I could quickly find a substitute.

To shake things up, I decided to go with someone more relatable to the students' generation, someone as different from Charlton Heston as Jimi Hendrix is to Lawrence Welk. Someone so far out there, even I wasn't sure what to make of him. His name? Frank Zappa.

The avant-garde musician/composer/film producer agreed, but he told us he was only available for his pre-taped segment a couple of days before the show aired. That was cutting it close, but I was convinced I could make it happen. *Just have to work a little harder and faster*, I thought. If Red Bull had been around in those days, I would've bought a twelve-pack.

On a chilly December afternoon, the cameraman, sound technician, and I journeyed toward Zappa's home in Laurel Canyon, the birthplace of the so-called "L.A. Sound." If you lived here in the late 1960s and early '70s, your neighbors included the likes of the Eagles, the Doors, and the Mamas & the Papas. Crosby, Stills, and Nash first met in the living room of the "Lady of the Canyon" herself, Joni Mitchell. It seemed like half the songs on the radio emerged from the area's zip code.

Once we arrived at Zappa's 1930s Tudor, a woman greeted us at the door and led us down some steep stairs. "Frank wants to do the interview in the Utility Muffin Research Kitchen."

"The what?"

"That's what he calls his recording studio."

I thought I heard the cameraman mumble, "Whatever floats your boat."

Like Zappa's music, the house's decor screamed satirical, whimsical, and complicated. The walls were covered with license plates, faded album covers, and a "Nixon for Governor" poster. The scent of tobacco became stronger as we neared what appeared to be Zappa's inner sanctum.

At the bottom of the stairs stood a tall, dark-haired man with a thick mustache, cigarette, and sly grin. "Good afternoon. So, whatcha want from me?"

We had previously sent Zappa some information explaining how the show worked and even some sample questions, but I was happy to go over it again.

"It's pretty straight forward, Frank. We're shooting a short, feature segment where you talk about creativity and offer any advice you have for young people who want to be in the world of entertainment. Then, this Saturday, you come into our studio and answer questions from a small group of intelligent students. We put it all together, and it airs on PBS a few days later.

"All right, let's give it a shot."

We sat him down in the midst of his "kitchen," set up a few lights, and began the interview. He seemed too laid-back, so I decided to start out with a question that might fire him up.

Frank Zappa and me in the "Utility Muffin Research Kitchen"
(Courtesy: KCET-Television)

"Frank, does competition have a place in the world of the creative artist?"

He took a drag on his cigarette then answered, "For some people it does. But the climate for anything creative in the United States has been very bad for a long time. People who normally do advanced things are discouraged, because they won't get it performed, won't have any way to bring it to the public. It's bad for creativity all the way around."

I figured it was a decent answer—might be a bit negative for the optimistic students—but I should be able to use it. Problem was, that was the *only* usable answer Frank gave. The rest of the interview went something like this:

"Frank, what advice would you give young, emerging creative artists?"

"If you want to get laid, go to college. If you want an education, go to the library."

"Uh, okay. How about specifically for those interested in the world of entertainment?"

"Get ready to work for brainless idiots, because almost everyone in the entertainment industry is stupid. In fact, there's more stupidity than hydrogen in the universe and it has a longer shelf life."

I did my best to persevere.

"How would you like to be remembered?"

"I don't care."

This is going about as well as trying to teach a cat how to use dental floss. Maybe a different approach will work.

"Okay, Frank, you're having fun with this, and there's nothing wrong with that. But I have a show that airs next week, and this isn't gonna fly on national TV."

Zappa took a long drag on his cigarette and sat up in his chair. "If you haven't figured it out yet, I don't like to encourage people to get into the entertainment industry. It'll eat most of 'em alive."

Would have been nice if he told us that before I hauled a camera crew to his house.

"But I do have some advice for the students," Zappa continued. "Don't do drugs. It just gives you an excuse to be an asshole."

I asked a few more questions, but, clearly, I'd have to find a different in-studio guest for the show. That is, if I ever wanted to work in TV again. I told Zappa my concern. He was cool with it. Probably even expected it. But the clock was ticking, and I needed a substitute, quickly. We couldn't go back and get Charlton Heston. He'd already been uninvited.

To my relief, the folks at PBS were understanding and came up with a timely replacement. Movie director Peter Bogdanovich (*The Last Picture Show, What's Up, Doc?, Paper*

Moon) may not have been a household name, but he was a master film historian and knew the business like few others. The students loved him. The shows went well, and an executive promised to have me host more of them.

I felt euphoric. I loved the intellectual atmosphere at PBS and envisioned the experience taking my career to a whole new level. But there are no guarantees in broadcasting. Sadly, later that year, PBS cancelled the show in favor of other projects.

At least the experience taught me two things: I knew I wanted to work at PBS again, and don't interview Frank Zappa—unless it's for an R-rated show.

# # #

After my brief but rewarding stint in the spotlight hosting *Why in the World,* my personal life continued to shine as well. Jette and I grew closer as she turned my bachelor pad into a cozy home and warmed up to my family and friends. Walter Cronkite's words continued to echo in my mind. *Solid partner. Through thick and thin. Someone who wasn't in the same business.* With Jette, I found myself checking off all the boxes.

Six months after we moved in together, we were engaged to be married. I hoped we could celebrate our engagement by attending Hollywood's biggest night, but it wasn't meant to be…

CHAPTER 11
AT LAST

March 29th, 1982 - Hollywood, California

"SORRY, KEN. No tuxedo for you this year."

Eight words I hated to hear. They meant I wasn't going to one of my favorite events, the Academy Awards. I always loved covering the Oscars. Hollywood's annual ego-fest meant mixing with pretty people, eating fantastic food, and viewing more low-cut gowns in one night than I'd see all year. But this year, I was out of luck.

"Need you on stakeout duty tonight," Bureau Chief Dan Bloom said to me on the morning of the big show. "Henry Fonda is up for Best Actor, but he's too sick with heart disease to attend the show. We want you to hang out in front of his house just in case he wins."

Fonda and legendary actress Katherine Hepburn were both nominated for their brilliant performances in the classic film, *On Golden Pond.*

"Better get there early. Those rain clouds look like they mean business."

Great, I thought. *Not only am I gonna miss the Oscars, I'm going to get drenched in the pouring rain, hoping to get an interview with a guy who might be on his deathbed.*

The show started at six in the evening in Los Angeles, in

order to air in prime time across the country. As the hour approached, cameraman Fred Williams and I loaded our news vehicle. We'd normally have a soundman, but they were all busy covering the main awards show. Fred packed the camera gear. I stocked the important stuff—coffee, chips, and a deck of cards, since it looked like a long, boring night was on tap.

We headed out of the TV City parking lot toward Beverly Hill's wealthier cousin, Bel Air—the kind of place where, if you have to ask how much a house costs, you can't afford it.

"You wanna cruise by the Kirkeby house?" Fred asked.

"Why would I wanna do that?" I answered. "Who or what is a Kirkeby?"

"You'll see," he said with a sly grin.

A few minutes later, my questions were answered when we drove past the palatial estate that played the role of the Clampetts' mansion on *The Beverly Hillbillies*.

After taking it all in, I said, "It's nice, but you know the old saying: money can't buy happiness."

"That's true," Fred replied. "But I'd rather cry in a mansion than in a shack."

Light rain fell as we pulled up in front of Henry Fonda's Spanish-style fortress, surprised to see we were the only news crew on site. Like many houses on stately Chalon Road, it was covered by ivy with a tall gate in front and a courtyard suitable for his-and-her Bentleys.

"Put your feet up. It's gonna be a long night," Fred said as he cracked open the deck of cards.

"Ah, the glamorous life of a TV journalist," I said with a sigh.

Well, this sucks. I could be schmoozing with the stars. Instead, I'm about to play Crazy Eights with a guy twice my age.

Soon after we began playing, we came under full military attack—at least, that's what it felt like. What began as a plink-plop on the windshield soon sounded like a platoon of tiny soldiers marching on the roof. We were being bombarded by one of those rare L.A. downpours that Mother Nature seems to give us every once in a while, as though to relieve her guilt over our general lack of rainfall.

"Well, if Henry has his own Golden Pond, it's safe to say it's overflowing," I said. Fred managed a weak smile at my bad attempt at humor.

After he creamed me at Crazy Eights for the fourth time in a row, the cloudburst let up. It seemed like a good time to stretch my legs and explore, so I strolled up Henry's driveway toward his black-iron gate. Sure, I could get in trouble for being on private property, but, as any inventive journalist can tell you, sometimes it's easier to ask forgiveness than ask for permission.

Through the gate's vertical slats, I spied a massive two-story, 1920's-era home overlooking the cement courtyard. Off to my left stood a smaller structure, which I presumed was a guesthouse or the maid's quarters. Both houses were white with red-tiled roofs.

Nice. Henry's up there somewhere in that big ol' house. Bet he's lying in bed in front of a cozy fireplace, getting ready to watch the Awards.

"May I help you?"

I jumped at the sound of a mysterious voice coming from somewhere in the pitch-black courtyard. Even though the utterance was that of a soft-spoken female, it's unsettling when you can't locate the elusive person in the dark.

I did my best to keep my cool when an approaching figure came into view from just inside the gate.

"Uh, I'm with CBS News. Sure hope Mr. Fonda wins tonight."

"Me, too. I'm Shirlee Fonda, Henry's wife. And you are...?"

"I'm Ken." Her gentle smile lowered my defenses. She appeared young enough to be one of Henry's daughters. "Nice to meet you, Mrs. Fonda. Didn't mean to trespass."

"Oh, don't worry about it. I told Henry the press might show up. Quite a rainstorm, isn't it?"

"That's putting it mildly." I glanced over my shoulder toward the dark street behind me. "My cameraman and I have been watching it pour for the last hour. Heck of a way to spend Oscar night."

"Oh, you poor things. Why don't you go get your partner then come inside and watch the show in our guesthouse?"

Don't give her time to change her mind.

"Wow! That's really kind of you, Mrs. Fonda. I'll be right back."

Her hospitable offer couldn't have come at a better time. The rains had returned with a vengeance. A bolt of lightning slashed through the sky, followed seconds later by a thunderous explosion.

KA-BLAM!

It caught Fred by surprise when I tapped on his window—he later told me he thought a tree branch had hit the car. "Hey, buddy, grab your raincoat. Henry's wife invited us in."

The veteran cameraman's eyes lit up. "Just gotta grab my gear."

Despite the downpour, Shirlee waited for us at the gate. If they gave an Oscar for generosity, she'd have gotten my vote. She led us toward the single-story house to our left—

a mini-version of the much larger Fonda mansion.

We wiped the mud from our shoes then stepped inside to find a comfy couch, big screen TV, and—best of all—a fireplace that flooded our faces with heat.

Shirlee glanced at her watch. "Got to go check on Henry. I'll send our housekeeper over with some goodies. Enjoy the show!"

As she darted across the rain-slicked courtyard to the main house, two thoughts crossed my mind:

First, Henry's a lucky guy to have such a caring partner in life.

Second, I forgot to ask her if Henry was willing to be interviewed after the show or if he was even healthy enough to do so.

Soon after the 54th annual Academy Awards began, Maria, Fonda's housekeeper, dropped by with hot chocolate and cookies. After telling us that Henry and Shirlee wanted to be alone, she joined us in front of the TV, where she shared some fascinating facts about *On Golden Pond* and her famous boss.

Jane Fonda had bought the film rights specifically so her own father could play her dad in the movie. The father-daughter rift depicted on screen closely paralleled the real-life relationship between the two Fondas.

The chemistry between Henry and co-star Katherine Hepburn created movie magic, but, incredibly, the two film icons had never even met before filming began.

And one fact that surprised me the most: despite a brilliant career, Henry had never won an Oscar. He once received an "honorary" statue, but, in my opinion, that's not the same. For half a century, Academy voters had snubbed the guy who tamed *12 Angry Men* and made *The Grapes of Wrath* bear fruit. Time sure seemed to be running out for voters to get it right.

We all rooted for Henry to get the gold, but first we had to sit through a couple of hours of the usual Academy Award self-congratulatory hoopla. The producers know, in order to keep an audience tuned-in, you put the most important Oscars at the end of the show.

Finally, the time came for the Best Actress award. Hepburn faced stiff competition from superstars like Meryl Streep for *The French Lieutenant's Woman* and Diane Keaton for *Reds.*

Actor Jon Voight opened the envelope. "And the winner is... Katherine Hepburn for *On Golden Pond.*"

Maria squeezed my arm. "*Whoopee!*"

Fred threw his fist in air like a crazed football fan after a touchdown. "One down, one to go!"

But I found myself more nervous than happy. *What if Katherine wins, but Henry doesn't? Probably best to keep that dreadful thought to myself.*

Moments later, actress Sissy Spacek stepped to the microphone. "The five nominees for Best Actor in a Leading Role are: Warren Beatty for *Reds*, Henry Fonda for *On Golden Pond*, Burt Lancaster for *Atlantic City*, Dudley Moore for *Arthur*, and Paul Newman for *Absence of Malice.*"

I pictured Henry and Shirlee snuggled in bed, anxiously watching as Spacek ripped open the envelope.

"And the Oscar goes to... Henry Fonda for *On Golden Pond!*"

Maria screamed. Fred and I high-fived.

When Jane Fonda accepted the Oscar on her dad's behalf, the joy in my heart became a lump in my throat. Her opening and closing lines said it all:

She began, "My father didn't really believe that this was going to happen. But he told me awhile back that, if it did, he wanted his wife Shirlee to accept the award for him. But Shirlee wanted to be with him tonight."

And Jane ended with, "And I know that, lastly but really first, he is thanking Shirlee Fonda, who has been his loving support for seventeen years, whom he calls his Rock of Gibraltar. Dad, me and all the grandchildren are coming over with your Oscar right away!"

When the elation died down, reality set in.

"I must go see Mr. and Mrs. Fonda," Maria said.

"Would you mind seeing if there's any chance he might grant us an interview?" I asked with a hopeful look in my eyes.

"If I get a chance, but I doubt he'll be up to it," Maria said as she left for the main house. "He's a very sick man."

Despite the pessimistic news, Fred and I knew our night wasn't over. Jane and "Oscar" were on their way to the house and, at the very least, we should try to get an interview with her. We kept a steady eye out for her arrival from the comfort of the guesthouse; no need to get soaked in the pouring rain.

A short time later, Jane and her family came through the gate. For some reason, Diana Ross, who had sung earlier in the night at the Oscars, was part of the entourage. Fred and I stepped out into the rain and strolled up to Jane.

"Ms. Fonda, can I ask you a few questions for CBS News?" I said, as Fred videotaped from over my shoulder.

Jane looked startled. Couldn't blame her. As far as she knew, we could have been crazed imposters who managed to scale the six-foot-high gate.

Jane Fonda (Courtesy: Georges Biard)

She whipped her head around and snapped at me, "Hey, how'd you get into my father's courtyard?"

"Shirlee was kind enough to invite us into the guesthouse to get out of the rain," I replied. "Can you describe how it felt when your father's name was announced?"

Just as Jane was about to respond (or, perhaps, have us shot), Maria came out and ushered the group into the main house. We were convinced we were probably going home without any interviews.

Still, Fred said what we both were thinking. "No use leaving until they kick us out."

When we retreated back into the guesthouse, I spotted other members of the media gathering outside the gate.

Damn, there goes any hope of an exclusive interview with Henry.

We downed the last of the hot chocolate while watching the post-Oscar coverage. After about half an hour, we were convinced Henry wasn't going to give us an interview. Then, a knock at the door. It was Maria.

"Mr. Fonda will see you now."

As if on cue, thunder roared like God moving heavy furniture in heaven.

We grabbed our gear and headed into the courtyard again. But this time, we knew our efforts wouldn't be in vain. Maria shouted over the pouring rain, "You're in luck. He's only going to do one interview." She glanced at the growing media mob outside the gate. "Maybe you can share it with them."

It might have been the magic of the moment, but the inside of the Fonda home felt like it had been designed by an Academy Award-winning set decorator. Henry preferred painting to acting, and his exquisite watercolors hung everywhere... still lives of flowers and fruit... a weathered ranch at dawn's first light. The calming scent of jasmine filled the air.

Maria led us up a winding staircase to Henry's spacious bedroom. Shirlee met us at the door.

"He only has enough energy to say a few words," she said in a voice barely loud enough to hear. "Please be gentle with him."

"Absolutely," I whispered. "And, by the way, Shirlee... I can't thank you enough for all you've done for us tonight."

I inhaled a deep breath and stepped into the softly lit bedroom. Propped up in bed, wrapped in a blue blanket, sat a bearded man holding an Oscar in his shaky hand. The one and only Henry Fonda.

While Shirlee pulled up a chair for me, I prepared to talk with the man who, at seventy-six, had just become the oldest winner of the Best Actor award.

"First of all, congratulations, Mr. Fonda."

He took a long pause then lifted his head and beamed those famous, piercing-blue eyes at me. He may have been sick, but his spirit came through as strong as ever.

"Well, I guess I got lucky."

"No offense, sir, but I don't think luck had anything to do with it. You're a great actor."

Henry faintly smiled. "I'm not a religious man, but I thank God I lived long enough to play this role." He took another pause to collect his thoughts. "It was also wonderful to work with Jane."

He shut his eyes and lay back on his pillow. Shirlee slowly took the Oscar from his trembling hand. I was sure the interview was over.

I was wrong.

"And don't forget Katherine," he said with a sudden burst of energy. "You know, she gave me that hat I wore in the movie. It used to belong to Spencer Tracy. I'm darned happy that she won as well."

I heard a crackle in his throat as he drew in a shallow breath and softly continued. "Yep, I'm a lucky guy."

I felt a hand on my shoulder. It was Shirlee's way of telling me that now the interview was over. I understood. The truth is there were *two* lucky guys in the room that night. I felt honored to have been allowed a few precious moments with her obviously very sick husband.

Fred and I said our goodbyes and headed out the gate. We told our fellow media members that they might as well go home, since Henry was done giving interviews.

I had no way of knowing how true that was. Sadly, he

passed away four months later. I have been told that our brief conversation was the final interview he ever gave, an honor not lost on me.

# # #

Coming up: My hairiest interview, a startling visit from the spirit in the sky, and why I don't advise smoking marijuana right before you do a story with the cops.

But first, this brief "commercial" break...

CELEBRITY SNIPPETS

ONE OF THE GUILTY pleasures of being a journalist is that you often get to see what famous folks are really like when the camera is off. Whether I interviewed them, worked with them, or just observed them, I acquired some fascinating insights about these celebrities:

JERRY SEINFELD: Told me the only way he survived the grueling work schedule of *Seinfeld* was because he did Transcendental Meditation every day. He also briefly dabbled in Scientology in his twenties.

JULIA LOUIS-DREYFUS: The all-too-rare combination of classy, funny, and self-effacing. Especially refreshing, considering she's not only a major star, but her family controls the billion-dollar Dreyfus Group.

GARTH BROOKS: Perhaps the most down-to-earth superstar I ever met. When I worked for NBC, he took the time to personally call because he liked a story we'd produced. He also volunteered to be in my high school reunion video. Fun fact: Garth met his first wife when he was a bouncer at a dancehall and had to stop her from fighting in the ladies' room.

ARNOLD SCHWARZENEGGER: Look up the word "narcissist" in the dictionary and there's a good chance you'll see a picture of Arnold. When he was governor of California, his people insisted on choreographing his interviews—down to the lighting, audio, and even the camera. When he finally agreed to appear on *The KTLA Morning News,* we heavily promoted it, only to have him cancel at the last moment. I'm convinced it was because "The Terminator" found out it would be live, and he wouldn't be in control.

STING: Humble and soft-spoken—refreshing for a musical artist of his magnitude. He seemed to take himself much less seriously than his public image would have us believe. We spent the day together, during which he checked-in with his wife at least three times.

STEVIE WONDER: I've never felt such positive energy from another human being. The man emits a happy song, whether he's performing or not.

ROBIN WILLIAMS: I once saw him slip a fifty-dollar bill into a tip jar at a coffee stand when he thought no one was looking. Says it all.

BILL MAHER: I might have caught him on a bad day, but he seemed socially awkward and humorless as he and I waited for a camera crew to meet us at his home. When the red light was on, he suddenly became a completely different person.

JOHNNY CARSON: There was an unspoken rule at NBC: You don't speak to Johnny unless he speaks to you first. He once joked, "I won't even talk to myself without an appointment."

CAROL BURNETT: She insisted everyone call her "Carol" and, without much coaxing, performed her famous Tarzan yell for our gushing makeup lady.

ANNETTE FUNICELLO: I was fortunate to spend an afternoon at her home several years before she contracted MS and found her to be incredibly warm and gracious. Of course, my opinion may have been influenced by the fact that I'd had the hots for her as a kid and the recently divorced Mouseketeer seemed flirtatious. My ego grew as big as Mickey's ears.

TOM BROKAW: Cold and aloof, although I was impressed when he told me he preferred to interview "regular folks" instead of the rich and powerful.

KATIE SEGAL: The versatile actress is best known for her roles on *Married with Children* and, later, *Sons of Anarchy,* but she told me that her first love was singing. She was a member of Bette Midler's backup group, the Harlettes. We also shared something in common—we both sang next to Bob Dylan at a recording session. She laughed when I told her Phil Spector "fired me" after a couple of takes.

RAY CHARLES: He's known as a soul music pioneer, but his favorite style was Country & Western. And, even though he was blind, he was an excellent chess player.

MILTON BERLE: A prankster even when he was off-camera. After our interview, the legendary comic decided he wanted my tie, so he took it off me and ran out the door. Since he was in his late eighties, it wasn't hard to catch up to him. I enjoyed the chase but let him keep the tie.

MISS PIGGY: Strangely silent when she's not on camera. For that matter, so was her partner, Kermit the

Frog.

# # #

Now, back to our story...

CHAPTER 12

UNFORGETTABLE

MY MOST UNFORGETTABLE interview of all time—
heck, I'll go out on a limb and call it my *favorite* interview of
all time—wasn't with a celebrity, a world leader, or a
bearded guru on a mountaintop in Tibet. It was with a hairy
female with big ears who insisted on hugging me.

Her name was Washoe and she prided herself on being
the first non-human to communicate using American Sign
Language. The adorable chimpanzee had fancy digs at
Central Washington University, complete with a
refrigerator, couch, toys, magazines, and a bed with sheets
and pillows—all well-deserved, since she had more heart
and brains than many humans.

Washoe could sign almost four hundred words, and
when novice university students came to work with her, she
would slow down her rate of signing just so they could keep
up. Folks from all over would come to watch Washoe act
out make-believe scenarios with her many dolls. She also
enjoyed painting and hosting tea parties. If she could find
time in her busy day, she even taught sign language to other
chimps.

During our "interview," Washoe proudly showed me
how she could brush her teeth and dress herself. For some
reason, she was fascinated by my footwear and signed,

"Show me shoes."

Her caretaker laughed and pointed out that much of Washoe's reading material consisted of shoe catalogues. Later, when she invited us into her "living room" for lunch, I was surprised to see that, in addition to her favorite cuisine of oatmeal with onions, she enjoyed a small cup of coffee. When her caretaker became pregnant, Washoe was captivated and loved to ask questions about the baby inside her belly. One day, out of nowhere, the young lady stopped visiting. Washoe couldn't understand why the most important human in her life needed to take maternity leave. Several weeks later, when her caretaker returned, Washoe gave her the cold shoulder, thinking she had been abandoned.

When the caretaker signed, "My baby died," Washoe understood firsthand the pain of losing a child. She had given birth to two babies herself and both died in infancy.

Washoe moved next to her caretaker, stared intently into her eyes, and signed "C-r-y," while touching her own cheek and dragging her finger down the path a tear might fall (chimpanzees can't shed tears.). The caretaker later said this *one* sign told researchers more about Washoe than all her grammatically perfect sentences combined.

I've forgotten many of my interview subjects over the years. But I'll never forget Washoe.

CHAPTER 13

ROCKY MOUNTAIN HIGH

ON A SPECTACULAR Saturday in June 1983, Jette and I were married in my parents' backyard by our good friend, Pastor Gary Golike. At that point, my seductress officially became my mistress. Soon after we returned home from our Hawaiian honeymoon, my mistress asserted her position in my love life by presenting me with a tremendous new job opportunity.

PBS offered me a producer position on their flagship news broadcast, the *MacNeil/Lehrer Report*. They were expanding their program to an hour and needed two producers to cover the Western U.S. The network had fewer viewers than CBS, but many considered their news coverage the most ethical and objective on television. As my mother called it, "TV for smart people."

I was honored, but there was a catch. We'd have to move to Denver. It was one thing to leave a secure job at prestigious CBS Network News after four years; quite another to uproot a native California boy to a place that's a thousand miles from the nearest ocean.

The offer sparked my interest for two reasons. With Jette and I charting a new path as a married couple, it seemed like the perfect opportunity for a new beginning in a different part of the country. Secondly, the news landscape was changing and not in a good way. Gone were the days of Cronkite, when quality journalism reigned supreme. Now it seemed to be all about ratings. In the past, CBS only had to worry about NBC and ABC, but now there was a new kid in town: CNN. At first, we didn't take the upstart network seriously. We even joked CNN stood for Children's News Network, Certainly Not News, or my personal favorite—Chicken Noodle News.

But CNN soon evolved into a more professional network and their ratings rose. At about the same time, ABC started to lure younger viewers with "flashier" newscasts. That's when CBS decided to shake things up. The length of stories was reduced to appeal to short attention spans, and style seemed to triumph over substance. There was also a shift away from straight news reporting toward more soft features.

In addition, budget cuts and rumored layoffs led to a general sense of anxiety throughout the once-proud news division. Programs like *60 Minutes* and *Sunday Morning* continued their tradition of high quality television but the jewel of network news was starting to lose its luster. I could sense many veteran journalists were becoming more and more uneasy with the direction CBS seemed to be headed.

I certainly was not in the same league as many of the network legends I worked with, and it was an honor to be alongside the best in broadcasting. But I started to think, maybe this was a good time to move on.

After a few days of soul searching, Jette and I decided to roll the dice and put Hollywood in our rearview mirror. We rented our home in Altadena to our good friends, Ann and Barbara, and headed east toward the majestic Rocky Mountains. We optimistically looked forward to our life together and a new adventure in a beautiful part of the country.

From my first day on the job, it was obvious I was going to be part of a major journalistic endeavor. PBS doubled the length of the program, renamed it *The MacNeil/Lehrer Newshour*, and provided us with state-of-the-art equipment. Their New York headquarters espoused a code of ethics that I wished every journalist would follow. It included:

❖ Assume there is at least one other side to every story.

❖ Separate opinion and analysis from straight news stories.

❖ Cover every news item with the same level of care you would want if the story were about you.

While I eased into *MacNeil/Lehrer*, Jette volunteered at a local hospital and kept the home fires burning while I was on the road. Denver charmed us with its contagious energy, gorgeous scenery, and welcoming people. Maybe it was the altitude in the mile-high city, but everybody seemed so happy (and this was before Colorado legalized marijuana).

But I didn't get to spend as much time in Denver as I would have liked. It soon became apparent that not only would I be producing stories in the Western U.S. but throughout the rest of the nation, as well. That meant constant travel. Right away, Jette didn't like that so much.

One week, I might find myself in Michigan, producing a sobering story on unemployment. The next, in Tennessee for an upbeat report on Southern culture.

In addition, I helped cover the 1984 presidential campaign and followed Ronald Reagan and his opponent, Walter Mondale, all over the country. I even found myself quoted in *Time Magazine*.

I learned something from every story I tackled on *MacNeil/Lehrer* and loved the variety. Time flew by like it never had before, except for one assignment—a trip to Arizona that ended with the longest night of my life.

CHAPTER 14
SMOKE GETS IN YOUR EYES

"KEN, WE WANT YOU to do a story about how states are cracking down on drunk drivers," our assignment editor said while poking his head into my office. "We're sending you, Rich, and Doug to Arizona, where they've got some of the stiffest penalties in the nation."

Rich and Doug were my favorite camera crew at PBS. With Rich's eye for flawless video and Doug's ear for perfect audio, I could always count on them to get the goods, no matter how difficult the story. We also enjoyed one another's company. When you're constantly on the road, your camera crew becomes your second family. You travel together, work together, dine together, and, if you're still speaking at the end of the day, you socialize together.

The three of us excelled at the socializing part. We shared a common sense of humor and nothing was off limits. Whether we found ourselves in a major metropolis or in Doodlebunk, Arkansas, we always found a way to have a good time. When you're three guys in your early thirties, trying to blow off some steam at the end of a long day, anything goes. Well, almost anything. I'm proud to say we adhered firmly to two cardinal rules on the road:

One, when we're working, the work comes first.

Two, when we're playing, we always remain faithful to our spouses.

On our first day in the Grand Canyon State, we met with victims of drunk drivers, visited several jails, and talked with a young man who had just received a lengthy prison sentence for his third D-U-I conviction. Our final interview of the day was at the office of Arizona Governor Bruce Babbitt, where we planned to talk about his state's crackdown on drunk driving. One of his assistants led us to his spacious office in downtown Phoenix.

"Feel free to make yourselves comfortable," she said as she turned to leave the room. "The governor is running just a few minutes late."

"No problem," I replied. I knew we needed about fifteen minutes to set up our equipment.

After the crew placed the camera, checked the audio, and adjusted the lighting, we decided to take the governor's assistant up on her offer and make ourselves comfortable amidst the regal flags, plush carpet, and breathtaking view of downtown Phoenix. Maybe it was the heady aroma of power in the air, because we got a little cocky.

It began innocently enough when we helped ourselves to some jellybeans off the governor's desk. Things escalated a bit when we enjoyed a cup of java from his private coffee maker. When it became obvious he was going to be more than just "a few minutes late," we took advantage of his private restroom.

Surely he won't mind... We're doing a positive story on his state, and he has been keeping us waiting.

Twenty, thirty, forty minutes went by. Not only were we restless after a day of dealing with convicted drunk drivers and their victims, we were also in dire need of some comic relief.

"I think I'll just sign a few bills into law," Doug said as he sank into the governor's sumptuous leather chair.

"My turn," Rich said as he took his place on the most powerful seat in Arizona.

Naturally, I wanted to take part in this sophomoric exercise, but I decided to take it to the next level. Not only did I sit in the governor's chair, I plopped my feet up on his exquisite, rosewood, antique desk that had probably been around since before Arizona became a state.

I could feel the history. I could also sense something else—a tall man standing at the door, staring at me.

Busted.

"Hello, Governor."

Rich looked surprised, Doug cracked a smile, and I felt like I had back at Eliot Junior High School when the vice principal caught a buddy and me swiping a Coke from the teachers' lounge. Clearly, though, the stakes here were slightly higher.

Fortunately, the governor granted me a pardon.

"Trust me, you're not the first to put your feet on that desk." He laughed. "My kids do it all the time."

Despite his kindness, I slithered out of the chair with my dignity in shambles. My sense of humor, however, remained intact. "I'm guessing this isn't a good time to ask you for a ticket to the Governor's Ball."

Once I collected myself, our interview went well, so, afterwards, I was convinced the rest of our trip would go just as smoothly.

I couldn't have been more wrong.

The next day, we had a pretty easy schedule—an interview in the morning and some pickup shots in the early afternoon. Our agenda allowed us some free time in the afternoon to chill. Since we were staying at the luxurious

Arizona Biltmore Hotel and it was about 110 degrees in the shade, the situation demanded we lounge at the pool.

We enjoyed a leisurely afternoon, relaxing and working on our suntans. But we knew it would be back to business at eleven that night. An Arizona State Trooper was scheduled to meet us at the hotel then take us for a ride-along in search of drunk drivers. The plan called for me to sit in the front seat alongside the seasoned trooper, a man who specialized in spotting intoxicated drivers. Rich and Doug were to sit in the back and record the arrests when we pulled over drunk motorists. I always got a kick, traveling with cops. I like the excitement of being in the thick of the action.

After we left the pool, we enjoyed a relaxing dinner then met up in my room to play cards. About half past ten, the room phone rang.

"Hello."

"Is this Ken Davis?"

"You got him."

"Hi, this is Cindy with the Department of Public Safety. Sorry, but we're going to have to postpone tonight's ride-along. The trooper assigned to you is busy with a crash investigation. Can we do it tomorrow night?"

"Sure, no problem." I figured the guys wouldn't mind. We could always find something fun to do with unexpected free time. Just have to spend another "tough day" lounging by the pool.

"Same time, same place tomorrow?"

"Sounds good. See you then."

When I told the guys the news, Rich said he'd be right back. When he returned, he pulled something out of his pocket.

"Wanna smoke this?"

Doug and I glanced at each other. We both knew it was a marijuana joint.

Why not? We're safely inside for the night.

Like many of my generation, weed and I had a casual relationship over the years. Back in college, I always thought the establishment secretly liked rebellious students smoking pot because a stoned hippie is a peaceful hippie. In fact, the only thing they are a threat to is the nation's supply of brownies. But, as my career kicked into gear, I rarely indulged. I needed all the brain cells I could muster.

We each took a hit. Then another. And another. I was no expert, but this seemed like high-octane stuff.

We were quickly overcome by a serious case of the giggles, immediately followed by a sudden attack of the munchies. Somebody cranked up the radio—Motown never sounded so good.

Just as we hit full throttle, a loud, ringing noise brought the party to a sudden halt. Through a purple haze, I grabbed for the phone—figured it might be my wife or maybe the office. I cleared my throat and did my best to sound clear-headed.

"Hello."

"Hey, Ken, it's Cindy again. Turns out the trooper wrapped up his investigation early and is available tonight after all. Can he pick you up in twenty minutes?"

"Uh, okay."

I hung up the phone and bit my lip. We were about to share a car with a lawman who, we were told, could spot an intoxicated person a block away, and we could barely walk across the room.

I turned to my partners in crime. "Gentlemen, we are screwed."

Our anxiety level shot up faster than a mercury

thermometer in the Arizona desert. No doubt we were the only stoned people in the entire state who were voluntarily waiting for the police to come pick them up. It felt like a slow-mo version of a Three Stooges movie. There we were, all three of us, stumbling around the room, crashing into each other, and mumbling like a bunch of malfunctioning robots... Must splash cold water on face... Must gargle with mouthwash... Must squirt Visine in eyes. It was all we could do to get each other on the same page and out the same door.

We swung by Rich's room to get the camera gear then stumbled into the Biltmore's ornate elevator. As soon as we reached the elegant lobby, we gulped down some complimentary coffee and plopped onto a comfy couch near the hotel's entrance.

"Breathe deep, compadres," Doug said as we fought to maintain composure. "It's going to be a long night."

Right on schedule, the trooper strolled through the swinging door. Maybe paranoia was kicking in, but he seemed to walk with a "you and whose Army?" saunter. I swallowed then stood up on my wobbly feet.

"Are you looking for the TV crew?"

"Yes, sir. You must be Ken Davis."

"Guilty as charged."

Brain to mouth: *Zip it. This is no time to be cute.*

Slowly but not so surely, we followed the trooper to his patrol car. With shaky hands, Doug placed a tiny microphone under the officer's lapel so we could record his interaction with stopped motorists. The guys jumped in the back and I sat in the hot seat—inches away from the stone-faced trooper. I hugged the door as inconspicuously as I could.

Try to avoid eye contact and say as little as possible.

We parked near a freeway onramp to watch unsuspecting drivers leave a popular nightclub district. A second trooper arrived to help with the time-consuming paperwork, so our "drill sergeant" could move on to the next arrest. Within minutes, we spotted a young guy straddling the centerline. We'd nabbed our first drunk of the night.

After that, there was a lull in the action. My brain felt like it was slowly returning to Earth. It appeared the Three Stooges were going to survive unscathed, until... the trooper turned to ask me a question.

"So, Ken, is this your first time in Phoenix?"

"Nope. I used to be a disc jockey at a radio station here."

"Really? What station?"

"K... , um, K... um. For some reason, I can't remember the call letters."

The sound of laughter erupted from the back seat.

"Wasn't it KUPD?" Doug said.

"Oh yeah, that's it," I replied with a nervous chuckle. But I wasn't smart enough to stop there. "I do remember we used to play that stupid song, 'A Horse with No Name' a lot. Never could understand why, with all that time in the desert, the dude never got around to naming his damn horse."

The trooper's eyes bore into my skull. "I guess that's supposed to be funny."

I don't recall much more of that evening, except that we pulled over several more drunks and I felt lucky we weren't ordered to join them in the slammer.

We laughed when we got back to our hotel, but, in hindsight, our "dopiness" could have cost us our jobs. The no-nonsense trooper might've decided to bust us for public intoxication, which wouldn't have sat too well with PBS.

Fortunately, he didn't do that, and I'm even convinced he had a sense of humor about the situation. When he dropped us off, he gave me a wink and said, "It's probably best if you boys call it a night."

# # #

Other than my sobering Arizona adventure, I enjoyed my job with PBS and earned so many frequent flyer miles, I gave them away as Christmas gifts. But it was tough being on the road so much during the first year of our marriage.

Then the clincher: Jette became pregnant.

Instantly, our priorities changed. The time had come to think of more than just ourselves. We were now going to be responsible for another human being. I vowed I would be around to watch our child grow up.

After a year in Denver, I defied my mistress and parted ways with PBS.

CHAPTER 15
CALIFORNIA DREAMIN'

BY THE TIME THE summer of '84 rolled around, I was out of work with a child on the way. But I wasn't too concerned. To paraphrase Helen Keller, "Security is mostly a superstition. It does not exist in nature. Life is either a daring adventure, or it is nothing at all."

We reclaimed our California home and waited to see where life would lead us next. I decided I didn't want to return to CBS. With a baby on the way, I wanted something less demanding that didn't require travel. That would mean a cut in pay, but a man must have his priorities.

So I took an assignment editor position at KTLA-TV in Hollywood. I only planned to work there a short time, until I got the "fatherhood thing" down. I ended up staying six years. But not one minute of it was more memorable than my very first day.

"I think this is it," Jette mumbled to me at about four in the morning. "I just felt another big contraction."

"But the doctor said the big day is at least a week away."

"Tell that to the newest member of the Davis family. I think he's about ready to make his grand entrance."

Like any diligent parents-to-be, we had previously packed our bags and filled the gas tank in our car. But there was a problem. In three hours, I was scheduled to start my new job as an assignment editor at KTLA.

It's no fun to call your brand new boss in the middle of the night and tell him you're going to miss your first day of work. But this was one battle my mistress was not going to win.

Fortunately, News Director Jeff Wald couldn't have been nicer. "No problem, Ken. I'll have Scott Barer fill in for you. All my best to you and your wife."

On September 22, 1984, at 7:01 p.m., Christopher Harrison-Banke Davis came into the world, weighing in at a healthy eight pounds, fourteen ounces. Looking at his beautiful face, I instantly knew that fatherhood was the most important job a man could ever have. In fact, nothing else even comes close.

# # #

When I finally started my new job, I quickly learned two things about KTLA. People tend to stay there for decades— a rarity in the broadcast biz—and it just might be the most historic TV station in the country.

KTLA was the first TV station to broadcast west of the Mississippi, the first to telecast live from a helicopter, and the first to use a mobile news van. Even the studios stood on hallowed ground. It's where the world's first "talkie" movie, *The Jazz Singer*, was filmed in 1927; where Porky Pig, the Road Runner, and that "wascally wabbit" Bugs Bunny sprang to life; and where future stars like David Letterman, Steve Allen, and Lawrence Welk honed their craft.

KTLA

Since both Paramount and Warner Brothers used to make movies on the celebrated lot, you could feel old Hollywood everywhere you walked. KTLA was even owned by an old movie cowboy, none other than Gene Autry. Most of the old stars were long gone by the time I arrived, but we still had our own family of colorful characters.

Our favorite "uncle" was Johnny Grant, the honorary mayor of Hollywood. He was a rotund guy best known for introducing celebs when they received their stars on the Walk of Fame. Always with a smile, he'd bounce around the lot, greeting everyone he saw with a vivacious, "Hi, Tiger!" The jovial septuagenarian holds a special place in my heart. When he heard that my father volunteered as a clown at the Children's Hospital of Orange County, he donated stuffed animals for him to give to the kids.

Our responsible but eccentric "older brother" was Gerry Ruben. We all considered him the finest local news producer in the country—and maybe the quirkiest. He'd painstakingly plot out each of his car trips, so he wouldn't have to make any left turns. The teetotaler once thought he'd gotten drunk because he ate a few grapes. And every evening, right before the news, he'd shriek, "Battle stations!" Quirks and all, Gerry mentored dozens of news writers, and his numerous talents brought KTLA broadcasting its highest honor, the Peabody Award, for the station's coverage of the Rodney King beating.

Then there was our "patriarch," Hal Fishman. As the longest-serving news anchorman in the history of American television, he reported every significant news event since 1960 and consistently topped the ratings. A voracious reader, Hal reigned supreme at live, breaking news, where he could display his scholarly insights for hours without a script. He was also afflicted with the most severe case of "anchor-itis" I've ever encountered—think Ron Burgundy from *Anchorman* or Ted Baxter from *The Mary Tyler Moore Show*, but with brains. *The Simpsons's* egotistical cartoon TV anchorman, Kent Brockman, was partially inspired by him. But no joke about it, KTLA thought so highly of Hal, they dedicated the newsroom in his honor.

I had a lot of respect for these three men, but I didn't want to be them—not even close. Johnny and Gerry never found the time to get married, and Hal seemed to live and breathe TV news around the clock. They gave their all to their mistresses—broadcasting was their lives.

By the time I joined KTLA, I demanded a more well-rounded existence for me and my family.

Stan Chambers with his grandson Jamie: two of the nicest reporters in the business (Courtesy: Chambers family)

I did notice one co-worker who managed to excel on both the career and home fronts—Stan Chambers. He became a broadcasting legend by reporting more than 22,000 news stories over his sixty-three-year career. Starting with the nation's first live coverage of a breaking news story in 1949, he was on scene for every pivotal moment in Southern California history. But, somehow, Stan was also on hand for something even more important: his family. He and his wife raised eleven wonderful children. I knew he was a great father when his next-door neighbor once told me, "I don't know how they do it. I've never heard a stern word come out of that house."

As any past or present employee of KTLA can tell you, Stan's talent was matched only by his humility. Along with my dad, he was one of the most honorable human beings I have ever known.

Emmy® courtesy the Television Academy

Thanks to Stan and the talented camera crew of Jon Fischer and Dave Moore, I managed to win three Emmy Awards and three Golden Mikes for best coverage of breaking news. But my biggest honor came when the man himself asked for my opinion about a script he had just written. This was like Ernest Hemingway asking for advice from a college English major.

I tried my best to help him, although I suspect he only asked to make me feel important. That's the kind of guy Stan Chambers was and the kind of man I wanted to be. A lofty aspiration for someone in the cutthroat world of broadcasting, but at least I could try.

CHAPTER 16
FOR ONCE IN MY LIFE

WHEN I BEGAN in the business, a grizzled, old warhorse told me, "Kid, every successful newscast must include a sexy woman, a lovable kid, an adorable animal, or a needy veteran. Preferably, all four. I like to call it my tits, tots, pets, and vets formula."

No doubt Walter Cronkite would question that philosophy, but it's true—those are guaranteed audience-grabbers.

At KTLA, my position as assignment editor required me to decide which stories would attract the most sets of eyes. I'd love to say journalistic integrity always came first in my decisions but, whether I liked it or not, one item was often an even higher priority—ratings. Whether it be news or entertainment, in the profit-crazed world of commercial television, ratings are paramount. In fact, anchorman Hal Fishman would call from home early every weekday morning to get the ratings from his newscast the night before. Since he couldn't have gotten home before midnight, I'm still not sure how he ever got eight hours of sleep.

Working in local news, I quickly learned there's another ingredient to add to the before-mentioned formula for success: crime. There's even a phrase for it: *If it bleeds, it leads.*

Murders, deadly fires, and the gold standard — a high-speed car chase — are staples of L.A. local news coverage. That's the reason local TV stations break into programming when some brain donor tries to outrun the police... the ratings go through the roof.

There's another brutal reality about local TV news that they don't teach in broadcast journalism classes. A missing pretty white girl from the ritzy side of town receives much more coverage than a murdered young black man living on the less affluent side of the tracks. This isn't a political statement; it's simply a sad fact. Remember the Natalie Holloway case? The disappearance of the beautiful blonde coed on the island of Aruba received non-stop international coverage for months. Think the same would be true if she were an overweight Latina factory worker? Not a chance.

Yes, like anyone else with my job description, I was beholden to the ratings. But, as often as I could, I tried to cover news items that had the potential to make a difference. Whether it was a report on the search for a missing Alzheimer's patient, a series on crooked auto mechanics, or a feature on "no-kill" animal shelters, those were the stories that made me feel good when I put my head on the pillow at night.

Meanwhile, the fire that once burned in my belly for news seemed to be shrinking by the month. Although I remained addicted to current events, I was no longer a full-fledged junkie. In the old days, even if I was on a hot date, I found myself switching on all-news radio at least once an hour to check in on the world. One time, after a concert at The Hollywood Bowl, I got in my car, immediately cranked up the radio, and listened to the headlines. Big mistake. My date angrily said to me, "I think you care more about the news than you do about me." My first thought was, *You're probably right.* I wisely kept that assessment to myself.

But by the mid-eighties, my priorities had changed. Now that we had brought a child into the world, I instinctively knew that no news bulletin—or for that matter anything else—takes precedence over family. I'd been too immature to realize that growing up, but I'd finally figured it out.

On a sizzling hot Sunday in August of 1986, I decided to see if I could go a full twenty-four hours without listening to the news and truly put family first. Even though I was on-call around the clock in case of breaking news, I decided to leave my pager behind and take Jette and Christopher to Raging Waters, a popular water park east of Los Angeles in San Dimas. Our good friend, Doug Walker, joined us, and we had a blast watching two-year-old Chris frolic in the kid's pool. After a while, we took turns monitoring Chris as we relived our youth on the various slides and rides.

Following a full day of carefree family fun, we had jumped back in the car for the ride home when Jette asked, "Is there something wrong with you? You didn't turn on the radio to check the news."

"Nope. Never felt better. The world can live without me for a day."

After dropping off Doug, we returned to our Altadena home where we were greeted by an unsettling sight: at least eight messages on our answering machine.

This can't be good.

I took a deep breath as I slowly pressed the *Play* button and listened to a series of messages that went from urgent to irritated to nuclear:

"Ken, call the office right away."

"Ken, there's been a plane crash. We need you to come in."

"There's been a mid-air collision involving a jumbo jet. Why the *hell* aren't you checking your pager?"

"Dammit, this is a huge story. Where the f**k are you?"

Aeroméxico Flight 498 had collided midair with a small private plane over Cerritos while descending into LAX. All sixty-seven people on both aircraft and an additional fifteen people on the ground had been killed in the disaster.

Coverage of the tragedy dominated every media outlet in town and the assignment editor for KTLA News was at home in his bathing suit. I told the office I was on my way in and quickly changed into more appropriate attire.

Fortunately, I got to keep my job as long as I kept something else in mind. It's okay to put family first, but, when you're being paid to stay on top of the news, you better do it—whether you feel like it or not.

CHAPTER 17

YOU'VE GOT A FRIEND

WHEN YOU WORK IN broadcasting, it's easy to think of your audience as a faceless crowd. But, as I found out one gloomy February morning, there are real people in that crowd who depended on me and my peers in more ways than I'd ever imagined.

While sipping cheap newsroom coffee and trying to stay awake, I picked up the phone on the third ring. "KTLA News. Davis."

"I want to die."

A spray of java nearly exploded from my mouth. "What'd you say?"

"My life is worthless," the caller mumbled. "Ain't got no reason to live."

At first, I suspected this might be a prank from a fellow journalist. Folks in my line of work tend to have a sick sense of humor.

But what if…?

"Let's try and stay calm," I said, inhaling a deep breath. "Did something happen to make you feel this way?"

"My wife left me, my kids don't know I exist. Nobody gives a damn about me."

After a pause, it occurred to me maybe he had reached us by mistake while trying to contact someone he knew.

"Did you mean to call KTLA?"

"Of course I did. I watch you every day. I feel like you guys are the only friends I got," he slurred under his breath through a hint of tears. "Sorry to bug you, man, but I just had to talk to somebody."

Holy crap, this guy is serious.

He sounded like he was about my age—mid-thirties, maybe a little older. Behind his erratic breathing, I thought I could hear the hum of heavy traffic.

Is he about to jump off a ledge?

"Where are you now?" I said, trying to mask the fear in my voice. "Maybe I can send somebody to help you."

"Nope. Won't do any good," he mumbled. "Probably shouldn't have called you. It's too late anyway."

Now I worried that he had overdosed and was waiting on pills to snuff out his life. "Well, I care about you, my friend. My name's Ken. What's yours?"

"Caleb, but they call me Cal. At least they used to— nobody calls me anymore. Are you a TV reporter?"

"Nope. I'm mostly a behind-the-scenes guy. Tell me about yourself, Cal."

As he shared his life story, I covered the phone's mouthpiece with my sweaty palm and tried to get the attention of my assistant, Dana. "I got a guy here threatening suicide," I mouthed.

"What?" she blurted, loud enough for him to possibly hear.

Juggling phone, pen, and a suicide caller, I managed to scribble her a note:

Quick! Get me the number to Suicide Hotline.

Once she recognized the gravity of the situation, Dana

could not have been more professional. She quickly flipped through the Rolodex for the number. While I stalled for time, a jarring memory crossed my brain. One of my roommates in college, Dan Hickey, took his life about a decade after we graduated. It still bothered me that I hadn't kept in touch with Dan. If I had, maybe there was something I could have done.

"Cal, you're not alone," I said, hoping he couldn't detect the panic erupting inside of me. "All of us have had times in our lives when things seem hopeless. I know I have."

Silence greeted me on the other side of the line.

"Cal, would you mind if I brought a professional on the line?"

"Not going to do any good. I just called to say goodbye to a friendly voice."

At least he's reaching out. Maybe it won't go beyond a cry for help, but I can't afford to take any chances.

"It can't hurt to try, Cal. I know I'd want that if I were in your situation."

"I can't stop ya," he muttered."Do what ya gotta do."

Dana handed me the number to Suicide Hotline. But there was yet another dilemma. I had never set up a conference call. A seemingly minor fact threatened to have disastrous consequences—what if I were to push the wrong button and lose him? Since this was in the days before Caller I.D., I'd have no way to call him back.

"Cal, just in case I lose you, can I get your phone number?"

"Nope. I've already given you enough information about me."

"Just bear with me, Cal. You know I'm here for you."

Mercifully, we were able to patch a calming voice from the Suicide Hotline into the conversation. A wonderful woman named Jennifer managed to convince Cal that he wasn't alone in the world, that people cared about him. I quietly listened for about ten minutes as she skillfully talked him off his precarious perch and even managed to pinpoint his location. When it became obvious I'd done all I could, I said goodbye to Cal. The next day, I called Jennifer to see how he was doing.

"I'm not allowed to release any personal information, Ken. But I can tell you this—he's in good hands."

I breathed a sigh of relief. Not only was I happy to hear Cal might make it after all, I somehow had the sense maybe I'd made things right with my old buddy, Dan.

In any case, I never looked at our viewers quite the same way again. I realized they were more than just a faceless commodity to be used for ratings. They were a community of living, breathing human beings, and I was a part of that community. They deserved the same care and respect I'd give a close friend.

For the first time in a long time, I no longer felt it was all about me.

CHAPTER 18

CH-CH-CH-CHANGES

IN 1988, JETTE AND I decided it was time to bring another Davis into the world. Since my job at KTLA required very little travel, I savored sleeping in my own bed every night and reveled in being a dad. The only thing that would have made it all the more perfect was to give our three-year-old son, Chris, a sibling.

This time around, we made sure we were better prepared. We wouldn't be moving a thousand miles away and starting a new job. Instead, I arranged to take a couple of weeks off from work to enjoy the arrival of the newest member of the Davis Dynasty.

On December 22, 1988, at 3:34 p.m., Philip Eriksen Davis blessed our lives, tipping the scales at a whopping nine pounds, fifteen ounces. I swear he had a smile on his face when he entered the world. Yep, we grow 'em big and happy on the Davis Farm.

KTLA anchorman Larry McCormick said it best on the news later that night: "Jette, you gave Ken the best Christmas present ever."

Meanwhile, while I paid more and more attention to my growing family, my mistress, in an attempt to reassert her control, tried to convince me that local TV was beneath me:

"You can do better than this. There's more money, prestige, and excitement on the national stage. Remember all the good times we had...?"

In 1990, I caved in to my temptress and quit my job at KTLA to become head writer for a new, nationally syndicated TV show called *Personalities*. Unlike news, these types of shows can get cancelled in a heartbeat. I knew that going in, so I had no illusions of job security. But it was hard to turn down the job—it was hosted by the brilliant Charlie Rose, whom I considered to be the finest interviewer in the business. Plus, it meant doubling my salary and even getting my own private bathroom, complete with shower. I felt like a kept man. Intoxicating.

Sadly, Charlie left after several months, when the show took a tabloid turn. I chose to stick around and, for the first time in my career, dipped my toe into the murky waters of celebrity journalism. Admittedly, I succumbed to the power of the paycheck. But I also held on to a little secret.

Early on, they asked me to record a ten-second voice-over announcement promoting American Airlines. In exchange for our running the promo on every show, the airline flew our studio guests to Hollywood for free.

The announcement went something like this: "Transportation provided by American Airlines. With exciting vacation packages throughout the U.S. and the world. We're American Airlines—something special in the air."

I didn't think much about it until reporter Sam Rubin (now with KTLA, where he's Hollywood's top entertainment broadcaster) pulled me aside. "You know, they had you record that so they wouldn't have to pay the performer's union fee. They figured, since you're the writer, they could have you do it for free."

I wasn't pleased until Sam told me the good news. "You're supposed to be paid $100 every time that airs. If I were you, I wouldn't say a thing—just let them keep running it every day. Then, when it looks like the show is nearing the end of its run, tell the bosses that everyone who's on the air must be a member of AFTRA (the performers' union) and must be paid their standard fee."

That's exactly what I did.

Personalities ran about another year. My short announcement aired almost 300 times. When the end was near, I joined AFTRA and presented a bill to my bosses for almost $30,000. After paying a fee to join the union, I cleared about $28,500. Not bad for ten seconds of work.

But the best part of working at *Personalities* was that I got home early and had weekends off. That meant more time to spend with my growing family.

#

With Jette, Christopher, and Philip

I also found time to pay it forward by teaching journalism classes at UCLA and USC. There's nothing like seeing a student's eyes light up when you help them learn something new.

More than once over the years, I wish I'd ignored my mistress and become a full-time college professor, like my dad. After all, education is in my DNA: my grandmother, my parents, and my sister all were teachers. And, years later, my son and two nieces would become educators, as well.

A proud pop with his boys

Then again, if I hadn't followed the siren call of my mistress, I wouldn't have experienced my favorite job of all time…

CHAPTER 19
GLORY DAYS

PICTURE A PLACE where, on any given day, you might watch comedian Steve Martin crack a joke in the hallway; have lunch in the commissary next to America's first woman in space, Sally Ride; then spend part of the afternoon watching The Temptations rehearse on a soundstage. And when you were away from this magical locale, you would travel the globe on somebody else's nickel. Oh, and one more thing—you'd get paid big bucks to do it all.

That place was NBC in the early 1990s—by far my favorite stop along my career path. I produced segments for the weekly, one-hour show, *I Witness Video*. Viewers sent in videotapes they'd shot of dramatic events, and we'd travel to wherever on the planet the event occurred and expand on the particulars.

It made for a compelling mini-documentary series. Initially hosted by Patrick Van Horn and then by actor John Forsythe, it aired Sunday nights at seven. If you don't remember the show, it might be because we were on at the same time opposite some "little known" program called *60 Minutes.*

Working at the West Coast headquarters of the "Peacock Network" meant I got to cross paths with some of the most talented folks in the biz. Most of them turned out to be pretty cool. Garth Brooks, Jay Leno, Patti LaBelle, Wolfman Jack, and Willard Scott all did comedy bits for my high school reunion video.

With Jay Leno (Courtesy: NBC)

I shot hoops with Branford Marsalis and the *Tonight Show* band when they set up a temporary basketball court in the hallway. And the notoriously introverted Johnny Carson took a photo with me minutes before hosting his final *Tonight Show*. The photographer managed to cut him in half, but I still treasure the picture.

Here's Johnny!

Then there was the time I helped actor Don Knotts search for his lost wallet. Much like his character Barney Fife *on The Andy Griffith Show,* he seemed as nervous as a ceiling-fan salesman with a cheap toupee. When we finally found the wallet under a seat cushion in the makeup department, I could see why he was so concerned—it contained at least a couple of grand in cash.

But my favorite celebrity at NBC was a jovial stagehand named Eugene Patton. He had shot to fame a few years earlier on *The Gong Show,* where he proudly went by the moniker of "Gene Gene the Dancing Machine." Decked out in his trademark painter's cap, bell-bottomed pants, and white sneakers, he tripped the light fantastic to Count Basie's "Jumpin' at the Woodside." Pandemonium would ensue as his shuffling gyrations sent everyone into an uncontrollable boogie. I always thought it was, by far, the best part of the show.

Gene Gene the Dancing Machine (Courtesy: The Patton family)

When *The Gong Show* was finally given the gong, Gene continued his stagehand duties at NBC, where I'd see his smiling face almost every day. Usually, we traded jokes and talked television, but he also shared personal anecdotes about his family and the old neighborhood. You see, Gene and I had more in common than just our place of employment. When I attended John Muir High School in Pasadena, he was our beloved custodian and a trusted confidant to every student he met.

When I wasn't mixing with entertainers, talk show hosts or my favorite stagehand, I got to work with some of the nicest and most talented behind-the-scenes folks in the business from Executive Producer Terry Landau, to future best-selling author Gary Grossman, to world-class cameraman Kort Waddell. Chances are you've never heard of Kort, but no doubt you've seen his work, since he's covered more major news events west of the Mississippi than any cameraman I know.

We had no shortage of stories to choose from at *I Witness Video*. Since it was the dawn of the home video camera revolution, an army of amateur journalists willing to send us interesting videos sprung up around the world.

I bounced around the globe, covering an avalanche in Norway, a rescue of beached whales in Australia, a scuba-diving dog off the Grand Cayman Islands, as well as stories throughout the good ol' USA.

I flew so much, I defined a good flight by what didn't happen:

I didn't sit next to some garlic-breath loudmouth who insisted on telling me his or her life story.

I didn't get stuck in the center seat between two perspiring, broad-shouldered good ol' boys.

Or, my personal favorite: I didn't end up bent over my legs, kissing my arse goodbye, while the plane took a nosedive to Never-Never Land.

I Witness Video sent me to Australia twice, and I loved every minute of it, except for one warm summer evening in the country's largest city, Sydney. After spending ten days covering stories in Melbourne, Perth, and Adelaide, associate producer Deedy Dizon and I traveled back to Sydney to spend the day with executives and journalists from one of the local TV stations. We had exchanged videos in the past and enjoyed a great working relationship with them. It's hard not to like people who utter phrases like "No worries, mate" or "Excuse me while I visit the loo to siphon the python."

After they treated us to a tour of their beautiful paradise on the Pacific, all of us met for dinner at an elegant restaurant overlooking stunning Sydney Harbor. Expensive wine flowed like water, and the menu didn't bother to list prices. After a sumptuous dessert, appropriately named "Death by Chocolate," the general manager of the TV station tapped his wine glass with a spoon, then rose to address the fifteen of us at the table.

"It is an honor and a pleasure to have our American friends visit our country. May we continue to work together in harmony for many years to come." After applause and a few more clinks of wine glasses, the well-dressed man continued, "I also want to thank our thoughtful visitors for this magnificent meal."

Huh? Did he just say I'm paying for this?

Deedy and I locked eyes for a moment. If I had known I was paying, I would have stopped at the appetizer.

I responded with the only answer I could muster...

"You're welcome."

What was I supposed to say? "Excuse me pal, I don't recall me saying I'd pick up the tab for this gargantuan display of gluttony!" The point was moot.

Thankfully, the money wouldn't come directly out of my pocket, but I knew there'd be some serious explaining to do when I turned in the staggering bill to NBC. When the waiter handed me the check, I did my best to keep my cool, downing my glass of cabernet to soften the blow. Out of the corner of my eye, I caught a glimpse of the number at the bottom of the check: something in the neighborhood of thirty-three hundred bucks.

"You realize that's Australian dollars, right?" Deedy whispered in my direction.

"Of course I do," I replied through a clenched smile with a false bravado that implied it didn't matter. Didn't want anyone to think the "big time American producer" was a cheapskate.

After the waiter swiped my credit card, I was relieved to see the exchange rate brought the bill down to roughly twenty-five hundred. I was also pleased to learn that Aussies never tip more than ten percent, if they tip at all. On this occasion, I followed suit.

When we returned to the States, I presented our coordinating producer, Barbara Stephens, with the bill. Fortunately, she understood, but she did find the need to tell me, "Next time you go out to dinner with a large group of people, confirm who's paying first. And if it's you, please try to see if there's a Denny's in the area."

"Yes, ma'am."

I Witness Video featured dramatic stories with no reporters, actors, or re-creations—only the actual people involved were interviewed. Sometimes, the events were tragic, but we always tried to find a way to educate the viewers and end on a high note. That's the case in these next two stories.

I've always maintained you can judge a person by the way they treat an animal. I have no problem remaining friends with someone who has a different point of view on politics or religion, but if I ever catch someone being cruel to a critter, things are apt to get ugly. *Very* ugly.

I've covered more animal stories than I can remember, but two, during my NBC days, will always remain close to my heart. That's because I'm convinced they saved lives.

The first story took place in northern Florida, near the Georgia border. Some say Florida is the only state where, the farther north you go, the further south you get. Unlike flashy Miami, this part of the Sunshine State is where country & western is the music of choice, pickup trucks outnumber polo shirts, and you're bound to hear colorful language like, "Well, that just dills my pickle" or "Y'all fixin' to go to the Piggly Wiggly?"

Northern Florida is also where one of the most disturbing videos *I Witness Video* ever received was shot. A man walking through the woods stumbled across a farm with nearly two hundred starving greyhound dogs crammed into tiny cages. Whoever put them there—make that whatever subhuman slimeballs put them there—didn't care that they were sick and lying in their own waste.

These once-virile canine athletes were veterans of Florida's dog-racing circuit. Capable of reaching speeds of more than forty miles an hour, greyhounds are one of the fastest mammals on the planet. In my opinion, when they're past their prime, it's up to the humans who made money off them to make sure they are rewarded with a healthy, happy retirement. But, of course, those humans must have a conscience—something clearly lacking in this case.

A video of the sickening scene later helped to put the animal abusers in jail, leading me on a trip to Florida to report on how more and more criminals were being convicted, thanks to home videographers.

Once I got there, I was happy to find that most of the starving dogs had survived. I also found a way to turn the negative story into a positive one. I came across a group of kindhearted souls who specialized in finding loving homes for retired greyhounds. I immediately decided to make their organization a big part of the story and even talked NBC into showing a toll-free phone number for people who might want to adopt a greyhound.

I hoped it would lead to some adoptions, but I had no idea how many. Greyhound Pets of America later wrote me: "After your program showed our phone number, we received the biggest outpouring of attention ever since we were founded. Our estimates are that 2,000 greyhounds will be placed in loving homes as a direct result of your story."

That piece of information impacted me more than I'd expected. It was then I realized how powerful shows like ours could be—not just for good ratings, but for good causes. I never forgot that, so, the next time an animal-cruelty story surfaced, I lobbied for the assignment.

The second story took place in Pittsburgh, Pennsylvania. When the rodeo came to town, some members of a local animal rights group snuck a video camera backstage and sent us some alarming pictures.

When I arrived in the "Keystone State," I tried to objectively cover the story by interviewing people from both sides. Rodeo organizers told us how well they treated the animals, and they even took us out to a peaceful green pasture, where pampered horses, bulls, and calves blissfully grazed. They did their best to convince us that their animals were born and bred to be rodeo stars and loved every minute of it.

The animal-rights folks weren't buying it. They claimed rodeos were cruel events where normally docile creatures were provoked into displaying wild behavior to make cowboys look brave. They also had more than words and pastoral scenes to prove their point: they had videotape.

On the first day of the rodeo, two women armed themselves with a hidden camera and snuck into areas that were off-limits to the public. The troubling images they captured included an electric prod being jammed into the neck of a bull as he was about to enter the ring; sharpened spurs worn by "brave" cowboys to deliver optimal pain to the animals; and tightly-cinched flank straps designed to make the horses buck vigorously in an effort to rid themselves of torment. The most graphic scene they videotaped was a bull breaking its leg while trying to throw a rider.

Rodeo organizers claimed their tactics were humane and injuries can happen at any sporting event. But city officials saw things differently. Thanks to the videotapes (and, I'm told, our story), the city of Pittsburgh passed a measure prohibiting electric prods, sharpened spurs, and overly tightened bucking straps. Since at least one of these implements of torture is commonplace in many cowboy competitions, rodeos effectively became banned in Pittsburgh.

Each of these stories earned me an honor that I'll treasure forever: The Genesis Award. The United States Humane Society presents it annually, "To individuals in the major news and entertainment media for producing outstanding works which raise public awareness of animal issues."

Since these awards represent saved lives, they mean more to me than the Emmys, Golden Mikes, or any other honor I've been fortunate enough to receive during my career.

Of course, all my time on the road with *I Witness Videos* meant I was away from my family. Unless I was out of the country, I did my best to not be gone more than two nights at a time and organized my assignments so I could spend as much time as possible at home, but the fact is I was gone… a lot.

I tried to reduce the sting of the job's demands in any way I could. My comfortable salary enabled our family to move into a larger home in upscale La Cañada, California, and enjoy nice vacations. And, if I did have to travel out of the country for business, I tried to bring back gifts from the places I'd been.

But, even though I made every effort to be there when I could, it was hard on Jette to remain stuck at home while I was off filming in some exotic locale. I told myself, "This is the price we all have to pay for living well," but I sensed my personal life and my professional life were on a collision course.

With all the traveling, I thought the time might come when I'd have to put my family first and leave my favorite job of all time.

It was a decision, however, I never had to make.

On a warm June morning, the *I Witness Video* staff was abruptly called to a "must attend" meeting. I thought it was to tell us that the show had been renewed for a third season. Instead, we were told the last thing anyone working in broadcasting wants to hear: *"You're cancelled."*

CHAPTER 20
STAYIN' ALIVE

AFTER MY FAVORITE job of all time closed up shop, I unexpectedly found myself out of work again, with a fat mortgage and four hungry mouths to feed.

The good news? I got to spend more time watching Chris and Philip grow up. They were nine and five at this point, and, more than ever, they needed their dad to be around.

The bad news? Since I was the resident breadwinner, I had to begin looking for work immediately in one of the most competitive industries on the planet.

While trying to decide if I wanted to return to local news, I picked-up three short-term gigs to feed my family and self-esteem. All involved some travel, but I knew they were only temporary until the right job came along. For the most part, they were fun and, in one case… fattening.

# # #

Who would turn down a job where you're paid to eat at the finest restaurants across the land? Certainly not me. I got to dine at top-rated steak houses from coast-to-coast while doing a segment on America's fascination with beef for the

Fox news magazine show, *Front Page*. Even better than being compensated for gluttony, I spent a week working with one of the finest broadcasters in the business—Josh Mankiewicz. Josh, who's now an Emmy-winning correspondent with *Dateline NBC*, is living proof that, first and foremost, a preeminent journalist must be an exemplary writer. He also has a hidden talent known only to those close to him: a wicked sense of humor.

Next, I was happy to get a less "meaty" gig. I wrote and produced a one-hour show for the Home & Garden Network (HGTV). Since it was all about the latest in home furnishings, we shot it in High Point, North Carolina—the so-called "Furniture Capital of the World." Thanks to Southern hospitality, I had a great time—well, except for one little thing. The show's hostess was convinced the show was all about her. She treated the camera crew like they were plastic lawn chairs in a room filled with expensive antiques. Once, after she'd berated the cameraman for something that wasn't his fault, he pulled me aside and pleaded, "Please let me film her out of focus, just so I don't have to look at her face." Fortunately, we completed the show without any furniture being thrown, but I made it clear I didn't want to work with her again.

My third short-term job found me writing sentences like this: "When she's not skiing down the Swiss Alps or sunbathing in Saint-Tropez, you might find her motoring through Malibu in her prized pink Porsche." That could only mean I produced segments for *Lifestyles of the Rich and Famous*. Yes, I freely admit I aided and abetted the multiple-g-force rise of celebrity culture and may have contributed to the dumbing down of America. But I told myself that Mike Wallace, Barbara Walters, and even Walter Cronkite once worked on entertainment shows. Plus, this job was a lot more fun than producing segments about drunk drivers and starving dogs, like I'd done on more serious shows.

I partied with comedian Louie Anderson, arm-wrestled tough guy Chuck Norris (he beat me), and attempted to match wits with philosopher Deepak Chopra (my loss to Deepak hurt far more than my loss to Chuck). But my favorite adventure was disco dancing with actress Angela Bassett in Acapulco, Mexico. Well, she danced. I gyrated like one of those obnoxious drunks you see at a wedding reception who clearly should have stayed off the dance floor.

With Angela Bassett in Acapulco

But Angela didn't care. Fresh off her role playing Tina Turner in the hit movie *What's Love Got to Do with It*, she turned out to be one of the most down-to-earth and intelligent stars I'd ever met. Raised by her single mother on the poor side of the tracks, she became the first African-

American from her high school admitted into the National Honor Society and went on to get her master's degree in fine arts at Yale. While in Mexico, Angela wowed all of us with her athletic skills and sense of humor as we filmed her parasailing, yachting, and dancing at the hottest clubs in Acapulco. But it was what she did off-camera that impressed me the most. She quoted Shakespeare, left her ego back in Hollywood, and never once acted like a "star." Angela made me think that maybe celebrity journalism wasn't so bad after all.

DISENCHANTMENT

*The broadcasting business is filled with
kindhearted souls who always place principles
before profits and only work in the industry to
make this world a better place.*

—Said no one ever

CHAPTER 21
WELCOME TO THE JUNGLE

Summer 1994

O.J. SIMPSON LEADS police on a slow-speed chase along Southern California freeways as millions watch on TV; Tom Hanks stars as Forrest Gump after John Travolta, Bill Murray, and Chevy Chase unwisely turn down the classic role; and my mistress and I are in the midst of a mid-life crisis.

# # #

My priorities had changed. As a family man, benefits and stability had taken precedent over excitement and fame. Meanwhile, the industry had become leaner and meaner. Budgets were cut as viewership was divided among more and more TV channels. Many of my friends at the networks were let go, and companies took advantage of the fact they could hire two eager newcomers for about the same salary they were paying a veteran like me.

When a new show offered me a healthy paycheck, quality benefits, and the possibility of a long run, I jumped at the opportunity. I had no clue that I'd soon experience a new low in both my personal and professional life.

# # #

I joined the Warner Brothers syndicated show *EXTRA* shortly before it debuted. The original plan was to feature solid, investigative journalism about the entertainment business. Unfortunately, the program soon morphed into a daily half hour of tabloid flash and trash. Highly paid and otherwise intelligent executives spent hours debating such "momentous" questions as:

Who's the latest celebrity to get busted?

Which stars drive the coolest cars and wear the hottest clothes?

Is there any way we can get more half-naked bodies on the show?

It wasn't exactly my idea of prestigious work, certainly not compared to where I'd been, but I didn't have much choice in the matter. I convinced myself I could learn to co-exist with this newest personality quirk in my mistress. It required volumes of tolerance on my part, but I soon found that enduring the extraneous fluff *EXTRA* put on the air was far easier than tolerating the drama behind the scenes.

I understand the environment has since improved, but, when the show started out, insecurity ran rampant. Co-workers were fired on a regular basis, employees were called names I would never repeat, and even an occasional shoving match broke out in the workplace. It was at this stage in my career that my hair started to fall out. Coincidence? I think not.

Fortunately, there were some quality professionals there, like Dana Adams, Rick Kurshner, Stacey Gualandi, Jim Forbes, Michael Horowitz, Jim Hunziker, George Moll, and Steve Saylor.

I enjoyed working with these people, but even the

pleasure of their company didn't make up for some truly inexcusable behavior by people who ought to have known better—like the supervisor who was given a free pass after calling a female reporter a disgusting sexual slur, or the senior producer so unable to control his temper, I saw him hurl a telephone across the room.

At *EXTRA*, my mistress and I had hit a new low in our relationship and I considered ending it. But because my family needed the money and benefits, I had to wait it out until I could assemble a reasonable escape plan.

Working on a daily entertainment news show reinforced my belief that stardom in and of itself is empty. You can't be truly happy unless you're nurtured by something deeper. Some of the loneliest people I've met were surrounded by fans. I'm far more impressed by the schoolteacher who spends their own hard-earned salary on school supplies for their students and by people like my father, who delivered meals to homebound seniors and volunteered at children's hospitals.

Of course, it wasn't all negative. There were perks from working at *EXTRA*, and my family and I made good use of them. Jette and I attended parties at the Playboy Mansion, and the kids enjoyed freebies like tickets to theme parks and sporting events.

On the job, I joked with Jerry Seinfeld, enjoyed a cigar with Milton Berle, talked parenthood with new mom Julia Louis-Dreyfus, discussed politics with Bill Maher, and skied in Canada with *Baywatch* actress Gena Lee Nolin.

*With Gena Lee Nolin on Whistler Mountain, proving there actually were
some good times working at EXTRA*

I also enjoyed interviewing two future superstars who
barely were a blip on the showbiz radar at the time: up-and-
coming comedienne Ellen DeGeneres and local-radio talk
show host Jimmy Kimmel.

Most of the entertainers were upbeat and fun to be
around. But, on occasion, things got a little dicey.

When boxer Mike Tyson was about to earn a whopping
twenty-five million dollars to fight again after spending
three years in prison for rape, I asked him at a jam-packed
Century City press conference if he wanted to say anything
to his victim, who was apparently living in poverty. One of
his goons jerked the microphone away from my hand, while
Tyson glared at me like he wanted to rearrange my face.

When I tried to ask comedienne Roseanne Barr a simple
question, she gave me a dirty look then snapped to her
brawny companion, "Make him disappear." It might have
had something to do with the fact that this was at the height

of her divorce from Tom Arnold. In any case, she didn't have to ask twice.

Then there was a rather unfortunate incident outside of the Los Angeles County Courthouse with Calvin Broadus, otherwise known as Snoop Dogg. When the rap artist was charged with murder (later acquitted), I was part of the pack of hungry media wolves who followed him and his entourage into the courthouse, all of us shouting out his name in an attempt to get a quick sound bite.

"Hey, Snoop, did ya do it?" screamed the guy next to me.

"Snoop, did somebody set you up?" a gal yelled from the back.

My competitive juices kicked in, so I joined the chorus. "Come on, give us your side of the story, Snoopy."

Everything came to a screeching halt.

Snoop's beefy bodyguards, my colleagues, and even the cops at the courthouse door stared at me in utter disbelief. How was I to know that only his parents were allowed to call him "Snoopy"? In the excitement, the name of Charlie Brown's beloved beagle just shot out of my mouth. I was both embarrassed and, admittedly, a bit scared. Fortunately, nobody went gangsta on me. In fact, after a few tense moments, Snoop cracked a smile. I think, if I ever encounter the guy again, I'll just call him, Calvin. Or, better yet, I'll just keep my mouth shut.

But no star encounter haunted me more than the one involving a celebrity I'd never even met.

CHAPTER 22
GOD ONLY KNOWS

"**CAN'T GET ENOUGH** of The Juice," our show's producer shouted with glee one spring morning in 1995. He was referring to O.J. Simpson at a time when the former football star was the most despised athlete in history. No matter. To the executives at *EXTRA*, he meant job security.

O.J. Simpson

Simpson's trial for the savage murder of his ex-wife Nicole and her friend Ronald Goldman produced the most coveted commodity in broadcasting—ratings. For months, nearly every night, our show opened with the O.J. story. It skyrocketed from "Trial of the Year" to "Trial of the Decade" to "Trial of the Century."

How big was public interest in the case? Consider what happened when the verdict was read on live television:

> ➤ An estimated 100 million people stopped what they were doing to watch.
> ➤ Volume on the New York Stock Exchange dropped forty-one percent.
> ➤ Even water usage decreased as people avoided using the bathroom (you know you have the public's attention when folks refuse to pee).

Leading up to the surprising not-guilty verdict, *EXTRA* had to come up with constant new angles to cover during the nine-month trial. Since there was often no real news to report, our staff had to get creative. Day after day, we investigated such earth-shattering issues as:

> ➤ Why did prosecutor Marcia Clarke suddenly change her hairstyle?
> ➤ Who tailors attorney Johnnie Cochran's fine suits?
> ➤ What kind of car does Judge Lance Ito drive?

Reporter Dana Adams and I were given so many feature assignments about the case, it became a running joke.

Dana would quip, "Hey, Ken, have you had your dose of O.J. today?"

Dana was a quality journalist and came from a hard-news background, like me. As the trial dragged on, it became more and more difficult for us to cover the daily drivel.

The highlights—or more like lowlights—of our assignments included everything from jogging with O.J.'s pal Kato Kaelin while he prepped for his upcoming naked pictorial in *Playgirl Magazine* to flying down to Cabo San Lucas, Mexico, for a feature on O.J.'s favorite party spots. (Okay, I enjoyed that assignment.)

After covering more O.J. stories than we cared to remember, Dana and I were given an assignment that hit an all-time low. It all happened in front of dozens of people and the good Lord himself.

"Ken, you won't believe what they want us to do this weekend," Dana said to me late one Friday afternoon.

"Let me guess. They want us to interview O.J.'s kindergarten teacher about his early fascination with knives."

"You're giving them too much credit. They want us to go to Nicole's family church and interview worshippers as they leave Sunday service."

The timing couldn't have been worse. This came after a week of particularly gruesome testimony about Nicole Simpson's final moments. The coroner testified that, in a surprise, nighttime attack on the front steps of her condo, Nicole was knocked unconscious then stabbed in the neck and head with a six-inch knife. When her friend, Ronald Goldman, tried to intervene, he was slashed more than two dozen times. The killer then returned to Nicole and slit her throat. That's the short, sanitized version of the slaughter—in court, every bloody detail came out.

Now, Dana and I were assigned to go to Nicole's house of worship to ask respectable folks in their Sunday best how the gory testimony made them feel. What were they supposed to say? "Gee, it sure feels good to know she died quickly. At least, she didn't have to suffer long."

I hoped for a major news story that weekend to cause our assignment to be cancelled, but no such luck. We met early that summer morning at the *EXTRA* offices and headed for the Catholic Church in Dana's BMW.

As we headed toward the freeway, Dana looked at me and said, "You know, God will get us for this."

I sank deep into the leather passenger seat. I knew how badly I felt about this assignment but hadn't given any thought about having to answer to a higher authority. "Really wish you hadn't told me that, Dana."

Dana and I went through a lot during our time at *EXTRA*. Our relationship was strictly professional, but we looked out for each other. I did my best to protect her when we walked through a yard filled with screaming inmates at notorious Folsom State Prison, and she always stood up for me when I dared to disagree with the bosses. Our shared sense of humor always got us by. But this assignment was different. Like children being dragged to the dentist, we wanted to be anywhere but on our way to that church.

We arrived to see a magnificent earth-brown steeple against a brilliant wedge of blue sky surrounded by puffy, white clouds. It was as if God wanted us to know this was sacred ground. Everyone was welcome there, regardless of race, creed, or nationality—everyone except pushy tabloid TV people in search of gratuitous sound bites from unsuspecting churchgoers.

"Hey, guys, we're over here," a male voice yelled out from the only other inhabited vehicle in a sea of empty cars in the church parking lot.

"Hey, John. How ya doin', Derrick?" I said to our cameraman and soundman, respectively.

"Wassup, guys?" John replied.

"I'll tell you what's up. My blood pressure," the

normally upbeat Dana said. "This has got to be the worst assignment of my career."

"Do we really have to bother these good people?" Derrick asked. "I'd rather be digging a ditch."

I was just as uncomfortable as they all were, but I had no choice except to play the producer card. "Well, we all need a paycheck, so let's get this over with. Church will be letting out soon."

Somebody mumbled, "Lord, forgive me." I'm not sure who—it might've been my conscience chiming in. With heads lowered in shame, we dragged our reluctant feet toward a cozy courtyard in front of the church. Dana and the camera crew stationed themselves twenty feet in front of the main door. A life-sized statue of the Virgin Mary kept an eye on us. Though I was as nervous as the rest of them, I knew I had the easiest job of all—I just had to keep a safe distance and look important. Unlike Dana and the crew, I wasn't in the direct line of fire, in case warfare broke out.

We waited in the Sunday morning stillness. A gentle breeze kissed our faces. A carefree sparrow chirped from a nearby pine tree. But we felt anything but tranquil. We sensed it was the calm before the storm.

Suddenly, two large wooden doors swung open and parishioners poured out the double doors ready to flood the parking lot. A smiling middle-aged couple led the pack— that is, they smiled until they saw Dana approach with microphone in hand.

"Excuse me, I'm from the TV show *EXTRA*. Did you happen to watch the O.J. Simpson trial this week?"

"Yeah, it was hard to miss," the man replied with a quizzical look.

"How did the testimony about Nicole's murder make you feel?"

The man paused. He took a long, hard look at the camera crew then turned his attention back to Dana. "How dare you ask a heartless question like that outside a house of worship? You are a pathetic excuse for a human being."

Well, this is going well, I thought.

Subsequent interviewees echoed the first man's sentiments. I don't recall every word, but phrases like "Keep away from my children" and "You're the scum of the earth" come to mind.

It didn't take long to figure out we were out-numbered and out-classed. They were right; our tongue-lashings were well deserved. These Christians had every right to feed us to the lions. After several more attempts, we admitted defeat and retreated to the illusion of safety in our cars.

"Sometimes this job makes me hate myself," John said as he flung his camera onto the back seat of his van. "We work for a bunch of idiots."

Dana and I waved goodbye to the crew as they gunned it out of the parking lot. We did our best to ignore the glares from the churchgoers while we hurried back to her car. We slithered into our seats, buckled up, exhaled. That's when things got weird.

Whrrr, thump. Whrrr, thump. The power windows started going up and down.

Bzzz, click. Bzzz, click. The doors locked and unlocked— at least three times.

Whoosh, clack. Whoosh, clack. The windshield wipers joined the show.

We both turned as white as the cross in front of the church.

"What the…?" I uttered under my breath as adrenaline pulsed through my veins.

Dana bit her lip. For the first time since I'd known her,

she was at a loss for words. In case you think this is normal for a modern car loaded with power options, consider this:

Dana had unlocked the door but hadn't put her key in the ignition yet.

Her hands weren't anywhere near any switches or knobs.

The stiffest drink we'd had that morning was a Starbucks latte.

When the noisy outburst finally stopped, in somber words, Dana said out loud what we both were thinking, "It's a message from above. God is not pleased."

I tried to ease the tension. "Maybe He's only having a little fun with us. You know, they say God has a sense of humor."

"Okay, God. We get it. We'll try to behave ourselves," Dana said with a nervous smile.

We laughed, but both of us were genuinely shaken. We may have started out for the Catholic Church, but we ended up in the Twilight Zone. Throughout our careers, we had faced plenty of earthly perils, but this took fear to a whole new level.

When we returned to the *EXTRA* studios, the executive producer scoffed when we told him what had happened. "Oh well, at least you weren't struck by lightning. We'll just have to find another O.J. story for you to cover tomorrow."

We just shook our heads as we headed out the door. Dana's parting words to me dripped with sarcasm: "Sweet dreams tonight."

After arriving home, I took a long, hot shower, hopeful I could wash away my sins. I'm not sure if I was successful, but I do know I will always feel unclean when I think about that day at *EXTRA*.

# # #

I learned several things at *EXTRA* that they'd failed to teach in journalism class. For example, in the entertainment news world, there are at least three different levels of truth:

One, It could be true.

Example: "*EXTRA* was first to learn that (insert name of celebrity here) will star in the latest *Batman* movie." If true, news like this is exclusive for about thirty seconds, until the star's agent calls the next television show to let them in on it.

Translation: it really doesn't matter who's first to know, because... who cares?

Two, It's probably not true.

Example: "You'll be stunned by what you'll see on our next show."

Translation: No, you won't, unless you're stunned to see that some actress has gained five pounds.

Three, No way it's true, but we're going to say it anyway.

Case in point: a story I produced about the star of a hit movie...

"Great stuff," one of the executives said after viewing my story in an edit bay.

Nothing like getting a shot of self-esteem from your boss, especially one who gives out praise about as often as Rush Limbaugh says something nice about Democrats.

He added one more thing. "At the end of the story, I want you to have the anchor say *EXTRA* is her favorite TV show."

"*Uh*, I don't recall her saying that," I replied.

"Doesn't matter."

Doesn't matter? When I worked in network news, an

intentional lie, no matter how trivial, would get you fired on the spot. Back then, we had specific guidelines to follow—with ethics at the top of the list. I'd already sold a bit of my soul to work in entertainment news, and now I was being asked to go against everything I'd been taught about journalistic integrity. I was being asked to lie.

On the other hand, this wasn't a guy I wanted to tick off. He was known for his quick temper, and it was an exercise in absurdity to disagree with him.

After a lightning-fast internal conversation, I tried to negotiate.

"Can we just say it's one of her favorite shows?"

"No."

The abruptness of his answer set me off.

"But that's a lie!" I blurted out.

His response haunts me to this day.

"It doesn't have to be true, Ken. It's only TV."

Fortunately, he stomped out of the room so I didn't have a chance to respond. Not sure what I would've said, but it might have sent me straight to the unemployment line—all over a lightweight lie about somebody's favorite TV show. It was just another *EXTRA* moment that grated on my skin.

In the end, I found a compromise that I could live with. I typed into the anchor's teleprompter, "We hear that *EXTRA* is her favorite TV show."

Technically true. We "heard" it from one of the show's executives.

I spent so many late nights at *EXTRA,* I considered setting up a cot to nap on while video vampires edited my stories. Often, I'd stay at the studio working until midnight, return for an early-morning meeting or interview, spend the rest of the day working on a new story, then start the cycle all over again. On-air staff, camera crews, and technicians had unions to make sure they received overtime and proper meal breaks. But producers? Forget it. We were supposed to be happy with our glamorous jobs and fat paychecks. Truth be told, if we added up all the hours we worked against what we were actually paid, the total on the bottom line wasn't as hefty as we thought.

All of us worked insane hours, but I was one of the only producers who had kids at home. I was also in the early stages of an incurable affliction that only gets worse and can be deadly in my line of work. It's called... getting older.

In most industries, you're just hitting your stride in your early forties. But, in the entertainment industry, you're equivalent to an aging athlete playing in the pros. The bosses treat you with respect as you get gray hair, but you sense they're always on the lookout for someone younger, faster, and, most importantly... cheaper. It's like being stamped with an invisible expiration date.

I did my best to ignore my fast-approaching middle-age and stayed afloat by putting in long hours at *EXTRA*. By the end of my second year, though, I started to crack. Something as little as snapping at other drivers on my ride home from work shot up a warning flare. That wasn't me.

But at least I had a stable home life—or so I thought.

CHAPTER 23
LANDSLIDE

THE DEMANDS OF MY mistress—my over-reaching career—spilled over into my home life. Jette and I started to have more and more disagreements, many of them over the typical things that parents have issues over, like finances and how to raise the kids. The stress of working at *EXTRA* only served to fuel the flames.

In addition, our conflicting cultural backgrounds sprang to the forefront. In her native Denmark, due to their sky-high taxes, the government picked up the tab for college education and most retirement needs. But here in the U.S., there are no guarantees. If you don't get an education and save for a rainy day, you can end up on the street. As a result, I became the "bad guy" when it came to things like saving money and pushing the kids to do their homework.

I urged Jette to consider part-time employment or at least job-training classes, just in case we ever needed to subsidize my income in an emergency. She eventually took a position as an assistant chef in a church.

In early 1996, after Jette had been on her new job for a couple of months, I sensed the wall widening between us. Mild disagreements turned into squabbles, squabbles became arguments, and arguments grew into shouting matches. Late one March night, after a particularly difficult day, the words sprang out of my mouth.

"Is there someone else?"

Her long pause told me the answer before she said a word.

"Yes."

I was speechless; couldn't wrap my head around it. I felt like I'd been given the death penalty for a crime I didn't commit—betrayed, shocked, and scared, all at the same time. Much of that night is a blur, but Jette later told me that I jumped out of bed and proceeded to pepper her with questions. Who is he? Where did you meet him? How long has this been going on?

The supervisor at her new job had swept her off her feet. The betrayal was so visceral that any urge I had to get her to change her mind was tempered by one simple fact: the trust had been broken, and, in a marriage, trust is everything.

The bottom line quickly became "someone has to move out, because we can't live together right now."

Since I was the parent who spent the most time out of the house by virtue of my demanding job, we decided it would have less impact on the kids if I were the one to pack my bags.

When we told our sons the somber news, seven-year-old Philip scribbled a note to each of us and handed it to us when we were done explaining. I slowly unfolded mine, afraid to face what was written within, and read these words that I will never forget:

I love you both, no matter what.

# # #

I moved from our beautiful La Cañada home to several different places before I landed in a low-rent hotel in nearby Glendale.

It was the kind of place where your neighbors included aspiring felons, rehab rejects, and folks with questionable bathing habits. But I figured I had better save what money I could, since I now had to pay both mortgage and rent. Ah, the glorious life of a TV producer—making a six-figure income but living in a two-star hotel.

However subpar my living conditions may have been, they paled in comparison to the emotional deficiency I lived with, knowing I wouldn't be able to see my sons as much as I wanted and needed to.

The lumpy mattress, the thin walls, the noisy drunken lovers in the room next door all stoked a fire in my belly. I was angry at the son of a bitch who'd seduced my wife while I slaved away; angry at Jette for caving in to him; angry at the world itself for not giving me fair warning that it was about to blow up on me.

When my anger finally cooled down from a rapid boil to a simmer, I began reflecting on what I might've done wrong to add to the demise of my own marriage.

Could I have been a better husband? Did I bring too many problems home with me? Did our cultural differences finally get the best of us?

I knew better than to think only one person owns all the responsibility for a failed marriage. It takes two people to make or break it. But I needed to know what parts, if any, were primarily mine.

I tried therapy, prayer, and long talks with those closest to me, but nothing seemed to help. My parents, my sister, and many of my friends were in happy marriages. I was the odd man out. The bottom line was that Jette and I were no longer in love, and our children were caught in the middle. It was, by far, the lowest point of my life. Like a skydiver whose parachute won't open, I knew I had to do something before I hit the ground—but I didn't know what.

Replaying the life scenario of work versus wife over and over in my mind resulted in three things I knew I had to do:

First and foremost, beyond work and my marriage, more than anything, I needed to make sure that the kids understood and accepted that *none* of this was their fault.

Secondly, I had to take a long, hard look at my priorities and rearrange them until they worked for my family and me.

And, despite what I was going through, I still had to earn a paycheck to take care of my obligations. But I was done doing so at the expense of my family and my sanity.

There was one more thing I needed to deal with—stress. I required some form of release, but overdosing on alcohol, drugs, or even chocolate ice cream didn't seem like healthy options. So, I relieved the equivalent of a bursting pressure cooker by taking it out on my mistress.

CHAPTER 24
MY WAY

"THIS STORY IS bullshit!" I barked one morning to an *EXTRA* senior producer who insisted I write some ridiculous story about the latest in fashions for pet dogs. He looked shocked—nobody had ever had the guts to talk back to him before—but I felt a euphoric sense of freedom. After a career spent toeing the company line, it came as a welcome relief to finally speak my mind.

I also took my newfound candor on the road when *EXTRA* sent me to Texas to produce a story about Anna Nicole Smith. The surgically enhanced ex-Playboy centerfold was in the midst of a court battle for her late husband's 1.6 billion-dollar estate—that's billion with a B. Never mind that Anna was just twenty-six years old and he was an allegedly mentally incompetent eighty-nine-year-old, when they walked down the aisle. Never mind that they never lived together and apparently only kissed a few times. Never mind that her wheelchair-bound hubby dropped dead after just fourteen months of marriage. Anna thought she deserved at least half his fortune.

While I covered the court proceedings in Houston, Anna's perky publicist approached me during a break, right after her client gifted the audience in the courtroom with third-rate acting skills on the stand.

"Isn't Anna holding up well under all that tough questioning by that mean attorney?"

Earlier in my career, I would have given a politically correct answer like, "Yes, it must be so hard on her during this difficult time." But since this was the height of my No More Mister Nice Guy period, I told her how I really felt.

"I think Anna's nothing but a greedy gold digger who took advantage of a sick, old man for his money, and I hope she doesn't get a dime."

The shocked publicist didn't utter a word, but her face turned the color of Anna's ruby-red lipstick.

Typically, being so outspoken would've been hazardous to my livelihood, but it didn't seem to affect my status at *EXTRA*. In a place where executives got away with calling reporters obscene names and stretching the truth on air was a rite of passage, my behavior was negligible. In any case, I realized *EXTRA* would only keep bringing out the worst in me. With my volatile domestic situation, I knew I needed something calmer.

Just as I neared a breaking point, my mistress must have taken pity on me, because I received not one but two lucrative job offers. The syndicated TV shows *Real TV* and *Strange Universe* actually got into a bidding war for my services.

But there was a problem. *EXTRA* had me under contract for nine more months. They had more power than I did. Every thirteen weeks, they had the option to renew our legal agreement, but I could only quit once a year. If I told *EXTRA* I had another job in the wings, I was convinced they'd keep me under contract out of spite.

I was screwed. They owned me. No way out. Unless… I could give them reason not to renew my contract. I didn't want to do anything criminal or crazy, but I remembered something I once told my students in a broadcasting class at UCLA: "The best way to keep your job is to make your supervisor look good."

Hmmm, the opposite must be true. All I have to do is make the boss look bad, and he'll want me out of here ASAP.

I opted to go for it. Since my contract was up for renewal in three weeks, time was of the essence.

The gossip grapevine flourished at *EXTRA*, so I started to blast my boss behind his back every chance I got. I hoped my words would get back to him and speculated he'd retaliate by not picking up my option. But, much to my dismay, he treated me nicer than ever.

About ten days before my contract renewal date, my hand was forced. Both *Real TV* and *Strange Universe* insisted I sign a deal or they were going to hire someone else. I rolled the dice and accepted the job at *Real TV*. Now I was the only one in the world who knew I was under legal contract to two different TV shows, and the clock was ticking. If *EXTRA* renewed my deal, I'd be forced to burn some major bridges and possibly face legal repercussions.

Time to step up my game.

As luck would have it, a golden opportunity came a few days later, when I saw my supervisor chatting with his boss from Warner Brothers. I overheard them discussing whether or not we could report an unsubstantiated rumor on the air.

I inserted myself into the conversation and loudly said to my supervisor, "Who cares if it's true or not? Remember you once told me, 'It doesn't have to be true, Ken. It's only TV'."

His glare told me my worries were over. Not only was my contract not renewed, I also received a fat severance check.

I started at *Real TV* the following Monday.

REBOUND

If you don't like the road you're walking, start paving another one.

—Dolly Parton

CHAPTER 25
AIN'T NOTHIN' LIKE THE REAL THING

Spring 1996

THE UNABOMBER IS *captured at his remote Montana cabin; it seems like you can't go to a party, wedding reception, or sporting event without hearing the "Macarena"; and my mistress and I are back in the saddle again.*

# # #

My cagey paramour made up for our horrendous relationship at *EXTRA* by finally giving me a job where I not only worked with great people but was treated like an actual human being. What a concept.

But there would be no rebound in my marriage. Soon after Paramount Pictures hired me as a producer and writer for their new show, *Real TV,* I came to the realization that Jette and I were going through more than a temporary separation. The time had come to quit feeling sorry for myself and man up, if not for my sake then for our sons.

I also learned a valuable lesson that I've never forgotten:

anger is a waste of time. Ralph Waldo Emerson said it better than I ever could: "For every minute you remain angry, you give up sixty seconds of peace of mind."

I didn't always live up to those words—hell, there were times I even yelled at myself—but I tried. I'll be forever thankful for the unwavering support of my parents, my sister Ellen, and my friends.

# # #

Since it looked like I would be with *Real TV* for a while, I upgraded my accommodations from Hotel Hell to the Oakwood Apartments in the Toluca Hills, north of Hollywood. This leafy, high-end complex appealed to the entertainment industry crowd with perks like a hair salon, dry cleaners, and even a rehearsal hall (I guess in case someone got the sudden urge to stage a musical).

Oakwood residents generally fell into one of three categories: wannabe stars, out-of-state business executives in town for an extended stay, or recently separated singles.

The wannabe stars liked the location because movie studios surrounded it. My fellow renters included character actors, musicians, and a plethora of "showbiz parents" who were convinced their little darlings deserved to be on the silver screen.

The out-of-state business executives loved it because they could explore the treats of Southern California on their company's credit card.

And the recently separated singles? Well, they were one part confused, one part angry, and all parts anxious about their futures. These were my peeps.

Since my mind had a lot to unpack, I found the

Oakwood to be the perfect place for a bit of R&R. My kids loved visiting, and the ever-changing cast of fascinating characters helped divert my thoughts from my crumbling marriage.

Yes, I had occasional mini-meltdowns—I never did pay back management for that towel rack I ripped off the wall—but at least I no longer lived in a cheap hotel where I suspected some of my neighbors listed their prior place of residence as San Quentin.

Another nice thing about the apartment complex was that it was just over the hill from the *Real TV* studio. Thanks to the witty and easygoing people there, I found myself looking forward to going to work.

The job was a no-brainer. I simply wrote and produced short, snappy stories gleaned from riveting videos sent in from around the world. Unlike *I Witness Video*, where we spent weeks working on lengthy in-depth dramas, *Real TV* featured quick clips of everything from rescues to explosions to good ol' country boys hamming it up at a hog-calling contest. It wasn't in the same league as the quality journalism I produced at the networks, but it was the kind of cushy gig I needed. Just what the doctor ordered.

Being a fan of cinematic history, I loved working at the storied location. You won't find it on many tourist maps, but Hollywood Center Studios (now Sunset Las Palmas Studios) is where Harold Lloyd created comedy gold in the twenties, Howard Hughes produced war epics in the thirties, the Marx Brothers ran amok in the forties, and television's Golden Age sparkled in the fifties. In fact, our offices were in the exact place where the first two seasons of *I Love Lucy* were shot. I could almost hear Desi Arnaz scream, "Lucy, you got some 'splainin' to do!"

#

But my good fortune at *Real TV* didn't carry over to my personal life. After I had been with the show about two years, it became clear my marriage with Jette would not have a happy Hollywood ending.

As she and I went through divorce proceedings, we did our best to remain amicable and avoid bad-mouthing each another in front of the kids. We weren't always successful, but there was one thing I made sure of—I talked with my sons as much as possible and never, *ever* missed a chance to see them for birthdays, school functions, or family events.

CHAPTER 26
COME FLY WITH ME

"KEN, HOW DO YOU feel about going to Mexico this weekend?"

It caught me by surprise when *Real TV* executive Danny Tobias asked me to fly south of the border. Producers rarely left town since we were needed at the studio to crank out pieces for the nightly show. Plus, most of our stories were short and usually didn't require us to leave the office to get interviews.

But this story was different. The higher-ups at Paramount decided that *Real TV* should be more than just eye candy, more than fast-moving video clips aimed at viewers who had no interest in overexerting their brain cells. They wanted us to include some deeper stories with more heart and soul. Case in point: my Mexican assignment.

"Why do you want me to leave the country, Danny? You trying to get rid of me?"

"Well, in addition to that," he said with a grin, "we want you to produce a story about American medical workers volunteering their services to poor families living in a remote area of Mexico. Out of pure kindness, these doctors and nurses fly down there on weekends and open temporary clinics to provide free medical, dental, and optometric care."

Finally, a story with some depth that shows there are still some caring folks in the world. Walter Cronkite would be proud.

"Count me in. What are the specifics?"

"You and cameraman Joe Guidry are going to take a private plane on Saturday to the Ojos Negros Valley in Baja California. It's in the middle of nowhere, east of Ensenada."

"Sounds interesting, but this hardly seems like a *Real TV* story."

Danny nodded his head. "I hear ya. All I know is that Paramount has ordered us to do it. Must be some bigwig's favorite charity. These people are as poor as the dirt they live on. No paved roads, motels, or even houses—just some rundown adobe shacks packed with agriculture workers and their families. Oh, one more thing. The place is surrounded by an ancient graveyard."

I looked Danny right in the eyes. "Let me see if I've got this straight. No place to stay, no road to drive on, and we'll be on foreign soil, surrounded by dead people. Have I got that right?"

"Yep."

"We're flying back the same day, right?"

"Nope." Danny's eyes averted mine as he went on. "You'll be staying overnight. You and Joe will have to sleep on the desert floor."

I took in a deep breath as I pictured sharing my sleeping bag with crawly creatures and possibly the spirits of dearly departed Mexicans. I'd been camping before, but the only time I'd slept out in the open desert was on the Navajo Indian Reservation during my college days. Let's just say, thanks to an unexpected thunderstorm and an abundance of firewater, it didn't end well.

Danny read my mind. "Oh, you can handle it. That's

why we pay you the big bucks."

Despite my initial misgivings, I began to warm up to the idea. It was a quality story and Joe was a fun guy. Plus, I hadn't left town much since the divorce.

"Okay, okay. You sold me. Anyway, I could probably use a little adventure."

As it turned out, there would be nothing "little" about it.

Just past dawn on a chilly Saturday morning, I arrived at El Monte Airport to find Joe waiting for me in the coffee shop.

"Did you brush up on your high school Spanish?" I asked.

"Sí, mi amigo."

Joe was the kind of guy every co-worker likes to be around. With his infectious enthusiasm, he always found a way to make work enjoyable. He was also multitalented. Even though he was still in his twenties, Joe was proficient at many behind-the-scenes jobs, from directing to editing to, in this case, running camera.

I whipped out my checklist.

"Sleeping bag?"

"Got it."

"Bug spray?"

"*Uh-huh.*"

"Loaded pistol in case of attack by poisonous reptiles?"

"What?"

"Just kidding."

We packed light since we were going to fly in a tiny four-seater. But I was able to bring along a cooler packed with water bottles, sandwiches, and some small toys to give to the kids in the village. I looked forward to seeing their smiling faces.

Joe and I walked across the tarmac of the small regional airport toward two men holding a handwritten "Real TV" sign next to a blue-and-white Cessna.

"Hi, I'm Dennis, your pilot, and this is Brad. He's a dentist in Sherman Oaks."

"Good to meet ya," I said. "You guys been volunteering your services a long time?"

Brad showed off his pearly-white choppers when he spoke. "First time for me, but Dennis is an old vet at this. This is gonna be the fourth time he's flown his plane down there. Should be a weekend to remember."

"Sure hope it ends better than it began," Dennis grumbled. "I got fired from my job last night."

Fun times. I'm about to put my life into the hands of a depressed pilot.

The four of us squeezed into the cramped plane. I sat in front, next to our freshly fired pilot. Joe and the dentist climbed in back. Soon, we soared across the San Gabriel Valley, above the towering skyscrapers of downtown L.A., then over toward the turquoise Pacific, where we hung a left and headed south.

Joe and Brad were having a good ol' time in the back.

"I've never been in a small plane before. This is fantastic!" Joe said. "You fly much closer to the ground than those huge jumbo jets."

"Where's my inflight movie?" Brad joked.

Meanwhile, Dennis was quiet—eerily quiet. Any questions I had were met by one-syllable answers. I found myself looking over occasionally, just to make sure the guy was still breathing. Like a computer in sleep mode, he was on but *not* on.

Quit worrying, he must be a good guy. After all, he's volunteering his plane and time to help the needy.

Somewhere over Catalina Island, Dennis finally broke his silence. "Even before I got fired, I could barely afford the payments for this plane," he mumbled. "Now that I'm jobless, I really don't have the money to burn for this trip."

Great, what's he gonna do next, turn around?

I decided to keep the conversation going, "So, what kind of work did you do, Dennis?"

"Oh, I worked for my brother-in-law in sales. All went just fine until his sister and I split up."

Well, isn't this just dandy? One of the reasons I wanted to take this trip was to forget about my divorce. Now I'm traveling with a guy who could turn this into a weekend-long pity party.

Jovial Joe came to the rescue. "Hey, why don't we all leave our problems back home and enjoy the weekend? I have a feeling we'll come back with a new appreciation for what we have."

To my relief, Dennis agreed. "You know, you're right. Let's have a good time."

Before flying to our destination in the desert, we had to pay our respects to the Mexican Border Patrol at the Tijuana Airport to gain clearance into the country. Many Americans think of "T.J." as just a place to party and buy cheap prescription drugs (or, in some cases, illegal dope). But, as we descended over the modern skyscrapers and massive factories, I was impressed by the sophistication of this bustling metropolis of more than a million and a half people. Dozens of major international corporations have manufacturing plants in Tijuana and more medical devices are produced there than in any other city in North America. In other words, if you're ever in need of a heart pacemaker or a new knee, chances are good you would find it in Tijuana.

After landing, we confidently marched up to a portly

immigration officer inside the airport's terminal. The guy wore a patch over one eye, and it's a safe bet he never skipped a meal. I figured he tipped the scales at about three hundred pounds. This was pre-9/11, so no passport was required to enter the country, just some ID and a smile. We figured it would be a quick and uneventful stop.

We figured wrong.

"Pilot's license, destination, and purpose of visit, por favor," the stone-faced officer said to Dennis in broken English.

After clearing our pilot for takeoff, he took a bite of his burrito and turned to Brad and me. "Identification, por favor." He took a quick glance at our driver's licenses, typed our information into a computer, and gave us the go-ahead.

Finally, he took a look at Joe. A long, hard look. The kind of look that a suspicious father gives to a teenage boy who is about to take his daughter out on her first date.

"I will need to see your passport, señor."

My normally coolheaded co-worker took a step back and raised his voice. "Passport? But my buddies just needed to show their driver's licenses."

"Passport, señor."

Joe let out a frustrated sigh. "I didn't bring it. I always heard Americans didn't need one in Mexico."

"No passport, no entry!" The officer motioned to a family standing behind us. "*Next!*"

Why would he let us into Mexico without a passport but not Joe? Did he not like Joe's sunny disposition? Did he not like the way Joe dressed?

Or maybe... it had something to do with the fact that Joe happened to be African-American.

"Are you kidding me?" I snapped. Granted, it wasn't the wisest decision to yell at an authority figure in a foreign country. No doubt, he had the power to send me to the slammer to bunk with deranged drug dealers or worse—a lonely hombre in search of a prison boyfriend. But I was incensed. "Come on. Give us a break. We're in your country on a mission of mercy!"

I wasn't sure if he understood me, since he didn't even blink. Meanwhile, a heavily armed Mexican federales officer looked at us like he wanted to introduce us to his buddies on the firing squad. Clearly, it was time to surrender. We weren't about to abandon Joe at the Tijuana Airport, so the four of us trudged back to the plane for our flight back home.

"I've heard of quick Mexican getaways, but this is ridiculous," Brad said as he climbed into our plane. "We didn't even have time for a margarita."

"I hope that racist pig chokes on his burrito," I said. "Guess I'll have to donate the toys I brought to Goodwill."

As we rolled down the runway, I heard an evil chuckle emanate from our pilot's direction.

"Screw 'em."

"What'd you say?" I asked.

"We'll pretend like we're flying back to the U.S.," Dennis replied with a sly grin, "but once we're outside the airport's radar coverage, I'll turn around and fly us into Mexico."

A voice chirped in from the back seat. "Are you out of your freakin' mind?"

"It's not as crazy as it sounds," Dennis responded. "They probably won't notice us, and, even if they do, they won't bother chasing us. They only have a few planes, and those are reserved for chasing hardcore criminals. They'll figure we're small potatoes and not worth the price of fuel. What do you say, guys?"

Maybe it was because we were angry about Joe being refused entry into the country or maybe it was because we were all in need of adventure. Whatever the reason, the vote was unanimous.

We decided to go for it.

My heart pounded as we hung a U-turn over the Pacific and soared south toward Baja California. We felt like smugglers in some action-packed movie, but there was no script and we had no clue how this drama would end. When I worked at *EXTRA*, I snuck into a private party to nab interviews with the cast of the TV show, *Frasier*. And, as a kid, I once secretly slipped into a movie theater. But this was the first time I'd ever snuck into a foreign country. I knew in my gut we were making a huge mistake. But, just as I was about to vocalize my concern, Dennis interrupted my train of thought.

"I've got good news and bad news. The good news is we should be there in about forty minutes. The bad news is a small plane is following us."

Busted.

It's one thing to be pulled over by a traffic cop for a taillight violation. It's quite another to have the Mexican federales in hot pursuit of you, five thousand feet above the Earth.

A river of sweat soaked my shirt.

"You don't think they're gonna shoot us down, do ya?" Brad asked.

"No way," Dennis replied. "They're not going to set off an international incident over a minor immigration issue." But the look on his face told me he didn't believe his own words.

Soon, both planes descended onto a dirt landing strip. The map said we were in the Ohos Negros Valley, but it might as well have said "the middle of East Nowhere."

To our great relief, the plane behind us turned out to be a group of American medical workers headed to the same desert outpost we were. I've never been so happy to see my fellow gringos.

"Just like I expected—adobe houses, old gravestones, and a whole lotta nothin'," Brad said as our plane rolled to a dusty stop.

"Looks can be deceiving," Dennis explained. "There's a massive underground water supply, and, depending on the time of year, they farm everything from alfalfa to watermelons. I think you'll be surprised—these are some of the happiest and most appreciative people you'll ever meet."

Dennis nailed it. We were greeted by hugs, laughing children, and even applause. I felt like a movie star walking down the red carpet, except we were hundreds of miles from Hollywood and our runway consisted of dirt and stones.

"This sure beats our welcome in Tijuana," Joe said, as an elderly woman embraced him.

"Unlike that border guard, these people know that human kindness is color-blind," Dennis said.

As the head doctor showed us around the makeshift medical camp, I knew I had to bring up the incident at the Tijuana Airport.

"You did what?" the woman shrieked when I told her that we illegally flew into Mexico. "I hope you realize that they can throw us all in jail and shut down our entire program!"

Great. Our little escapade could threaten the health of hundreds of people.

She let that horrible thought sink in for a beat then let

out a little smile.

"Just messin' with ya. Did the immigration agent happen to look like a beached whale with an eye patch?"

"That's the guy."

"We should have warned you about him," she said as she shook her head. "They have at least a dozen immigration agents at that airport, and he's the only one who gives us trouble. He was trying to get a bribe out of you. I suspect it was more about greed than racism."

I let out a sigh of relief. "So does that mean we're in the clear?"

"Well, you're the first Americans I've ever met who snuck into Mexico. Usually, it's the other way around. My guess is nothing will happen, but I can't say for sure. However, there is one thing I do know for certain."

"What's that?"

"You guys have got a healthy set of cojones." If laughter is the best medicine, I'd found the right doctor.

We spent the rest of the day watching in awe as fifteen doctors and nurses tirelessly treated several hundred farmworkers and their families. Everyone from expectant mothers to elderly men lined up in the desert heat. I figured this was the first time many of them had received professional medical care.

When we weren't videotaping our story, Joe and I had a blast playing with the kids. They loved the toys I'd brought. But my partner was the star of the show when he taught them how to use his fancy camera that probably cost more than their parents made in a year. The children's pure, uninhibited joy helped bury a numbing thought that burned in the back of both of our minds: What if the Mexican authorities ask the U.S. Border Patrol to detain us when we return to the States?

Once again, Joe's positive outlook shined through. "Whatever happens, this trip was worth it."

Our night sleeping under the majestic Mexican sky only added to the adventure. Even though it started to drizzle, Joe and I volunteered to sleep out in the open, since it was too crowded for everyone to fit under shelter. To avoid the rain, we slept under our plane's small wings. Thankfully, neither creepy critters nor scary spirits from the nearby graveyard disturbed our slumber.

The next day, we shot the final interviews for our story and prepared to leave. The residents of the Ohos Negros Valley couldn't have been more appreciative to all of us, but Joe and I knew the only heroes were the doctors and nurses who'd volunteered their time and expertise. All we did was document acts of human kindness and play with the kids. It was one of the most gratifying stories I ever covered.

However, once we were en route home, there was another little matter to consider. Would we be handcuffed and sent back to Mexico to face charges?

To our relief, our stop at U.S. Customs near San Diego went as smooth as a shot of the finest Mexican tequila.

Our story aired about two weeks later and led to more medical workers taking their talents south of the border. I'm also happy to report that Dennis soon found a new job, Brad continued to volunteer his dental services, and Joe went on to have a sterling career that's taken him all over the globe, directing reality TV shows.

No word on what happened to the beached whale with an eye patch.

CHAPTER 27

VIVA LAS VEGAS

FOR THE FIRST TWO years after Jette and I divorced, I didn't get involved in the dating scene. My children had been through enough. The time wasn't right for them to see their dad with another woman. The money I saved from not dating went toward quality vacations with my sons. When I eventually did get back in the game, it was like buying a lottery ticket. At first glance, I'd get my hopes up. But when I scratched away at the surface, rarely did I find a winner. Sure, it was fun to flirt again, and I met some interesting ladies, but there were also dates when I faked a smile and thought, *Please God, let there be an earthquake, so I can run for cover.*

One Friday in May of 1999, when I was particularly discouraged about my love life, I made a spur-of-the-moment decision to shake things up and head to Las Vegas. That night, I boarded a flight to Sin City, determined to do something rare: spend an entire weekend hanging out with myself.

The first night went fine. I treated myself to a delicious dinner, won a bit on the slots, and enjoyed life's simple pleasures at a hokey comedy show.

This being alone thing isn't so bad.

Saturday, I enjoyed lounging by the pool but grew tired of laughing at my own corny jokes and arguing with myself over which show I wanted to see. That night, I learned that sharing the thrill of Cirque du Soleil with strangers from Syracuse isn't quite the same as experiencing it with a loved one. But at least it was easier and cheaper to get a good seat, since I only needed one.

By Sunday, I was thoroughly sick and tired of myself. I threw on my last clean shirt, didn't shave, and barely brushed my teeth. I looked in the mirror and shook my head.

Why did I waste my precious weekend alone in this crass cradle of greed when I could have spent it at the beach with a good book?

I had one mission on my mind: get to the airport and catch my flight back home. But when I arrived at the Southwest Airlines gate, my flight to Burbank had been delayed an hour. Fidgety and bored, I wandered over to a set of one-armed bandits that stood ready to steal people's last quarters before they left town.

After a few unsuccessful spins, I got in line for my plane. I was on the seven o'clock flight, but since it was running late, passengers for the next scheduled departure were also lining-up. In the confusion, I found myself standing next to two pretty women who were on the later flight.

The blonde to my left spoke first. "Hi, I'm Leanne."

"And I'm Carole," her brown-haired friend piped in.

"I'm Ken. Nice to meet you." I locked eyes with Carole.

Maybe this trip is going to be worthwhile after all.

There was just one problem. Thanks to my questionable hygiene and downbeat mood, I was hardly in top form. After some general pleasantries, Carole asked me what I did for a living.

"Oh, I'm a TV producer."

Leanne looked at me like I was O.J. Simpson and she was prosecuting attorney Marcia Clarke.

"Sure you are," she said in a voice that told me she didn't believe a word I said.

"Do you have a business card?" Carole asked.

"Of course," I replied, confidently whipping out my wallet.

Driver's license, pictures of my kids, credit card, even a crumpled Keno ticket, but no business card. I'd been meaning to restock but had failed to do so. I began to sweat.

"I guess you'll just have to trust me."

Fortunately, Carole thought I was worth taking a chance on. She was smart enough not to give her contact information to a stranger, but she took mine and promised to call. I gave her my work number to lend credence to my claim of being a TV producer. She phoned the next day, and we enjoyed a fantastic first date a few nights later.

It turned out I hit the jackpot in Vegas after all.

But after many months of dating Carole, I still hadn't told my sons about my budding romance. I was bound and determined that that wasn't going to happen until I knew she was "the one."

Carole and me in our dating days

Later that year, when Chris was a sophomore in high school, he moved into my house in South Pasadena. It was wonderful living with my oldest son during his high school days. Soon the time came for both him and Philip to meet Carole. To my relief, they instantly connected. For the first time in a long time, both my personal and professional life co-existed peacefully. They liked me at *Real TV* and loved me at home. How could anything possibly go wrong?

Leave it to my mistress to find a way.

CHAPTER 28
(JUST LIKE) STARTING OVER

DESPITE *REAL TV'S* solid ratings, the executives at Paramount couldn't leave well enough alone. They replaced our likable and talented host, John Daly, with a retired pro-football player who managed to fumble away our audience. In 2001, *Real TV* was cancelled, and I was out of work yet again. But I couldn't complain. A five-year run for a TV show is like your pet living into its teens: you're just grateful it had a long life.

I was confident that I'd find work in no time at all. Who wouldn't want to hire a nice guy like me, who had numerous awards and decades of experience?

It turns out—a lot of people.

I didn't take it personally. There were only so many broadcasting jobs out there. None of my buddies in the business knew of any openings, so I had to hit the interview circuit—a humbling experience for a grizzled veteran of the business like me.

One such interrogation was with a young executive whose facial expressions told me he'd rather be playing Xbox. The job interview went something like this:

Him: "Your resume says you worked on *The Real World*."

Me: "*Uh*, that would be *Real TV.*"

Him: "Are you sure?"

Me: "*Uh*, pretty sure. I worked there for five years."

Him: "If you say so. Anyway, I've always wanted to work on *The Real World*. Do you know anybody over there who can get me a job?"

Me: "I don't think so. That's an MTV show. I worked for Paramount."

Him: "Too bad. Anyway, we'll be in touch."

They weren't.

Fortunately, I was able to pick up freelance work on the side. My first gig was with the VH1 network, where I wrote and produced a few segments for the series, *Behind The Music.*

Next, I was hired to produce a documentary for The Travel Channel. No, it wasn't about the enchanting inns of New England or the best beaches on Bali. It focused on notorious murders in prominent areas of the country.

Here's how they promoted it in a press release:

CRIME SCENE SECRETS: FAMOUS PLACES, INFAMOUS CASES

Three world-renowned destinations in three entirely different environments have something in common: each has been held hostage by a killer. In Yosemite National Park, a handyman snuffs out the lives of four nature lovers. Then, a world away, in Miami's glitzy South Beach, a serial killer sets his sights on fashion superstar Gianni Versace.

And in the 1960s, when a mysterious "Boston Strangler" murders thirteen women, a construction

*worker named Albert DeSalvo confesses to the
crimes. His story holds for 40 years, until the nephew
of one of his alleged victims asks if DeSalvo is really
the Boston Strangler. Now, Casey Sherman is on a
mission to find the true killer of his aunt, Mary
Sullivan. Through the eyes of those who can never
forget, we explore new revelations about three of
America's most notorious crimes... on Crime Scene
Secrets: Famous Places, Infamous Cases.*

The documentary's macabre subject matter brought
back *warm and fuzzy* memories of another story earlier in my
career—the Hillside Strangler case. Meanwhile, I continued
my proud tradition of doing my best to have a good time
while on the road.

In Boston, the local camera crew introduced me to some
of the finest Italian food on the planet, and I found time to
brush up on my American history on the Freedom Trail. In
Miami, I visited Versace's favorite hangouts and filmed
inside the untamed discos of South Beach.

In Yosemite National Park, I not only got to breathe in
the spectacular scenery, I also brought Carole along to be
my production assistant. She did such an exemplary job, I
upgraded her on the spot to a "starring role." When we shot
a re-creation of the killer handyman chasing a woman
through the woods, Carole played the part of the desperate
victim. Even though there were more close-ups of her feet
than her face, she gave an award-worthy performance.

In the summer of 2001, Carole moved in with Chris and
me. We resettled into a larger home, she got a nearby job,
and we added a feisty terrier named Buckley to the mix. It
felt good to have a feeling of family again.

And what about my mistress? Well, surprisingly, she'd been playing nice. She even led me back to our old stomping grounds.

CHAPTER 29
HERE COMES THE SUN

"**WELCOME BACK, KEN,**" Stan Chambers said to me as I returned to KTLA after an eleven-year absence. "You're not gonna recognize the place."

The legendary reporter was right. The news staff had nearly tripled since I left in 1990 to work with Charlie Rose on the show, *Personalities*. Even Stan's talented grandson, Jamie Chambers, had joined the team. The expansion was mostly due to the addition of the *KTLA Morning News*. It went on to become the highest-rated local morning show in the country, but things haven't always been so rosy.

When the blend of news, entertainment, weather, and traffic premiered in the early nineties, *Good Morning Bakersfield* probably had more viewers. Okay, it wasn't that bad, but network programs like *The Today Show* and *Good Morning America* clobbered KTLA in the ratings. As a result, the new show had trouble getting A-list guests, and, when they did, the stars sometimes cancelled at the last minute to take a higher profile booking on one of the network shows.

Just when the *KTLA Morning News* appeared to be on the verge of cancellation, a television programming genius named Joel Tator took the reins. I first met Joel while I was still a TV anchorman in Arizona in the seventies. When I visited home, he was kind enough to invite me to NBC to watch him *direct The Tomorrow Show* with Tom Snyder. Later, at KNXT, he hired me to produce a few segments for his innovative feature show, *2 on the Town.*

When Joel came on board, his plan to save KTLA's sinking ship was simple: everybody loves an underdog, why not embrace it?

The anchors loosened up and made light of everything, from their low ratings to the cheap news desk that looked like it came from a garage sale. They even joked on the air about memos from the front office ordering them to cut back on expenses. But when major news broke, it was all business. Quality journalists like Carlos Amezcua, Barbara Beck, Sam Rubin, and Eric Spillman proved they could be not only likable personalities, but also first-rate reporters. Viewers began to root for them, and the show has ruled the ratings in Southern California ever since.

I particularly enjoyed getting to meet guests who were at the top of their field, whether it be in entertainment, politics, academia, or simply ordinary people who had done extraordinary things.

Tom Brokaw

With two former mayors of L.A., "pondering the future of the city"

Former Los Angeles Mayor Antonio Villaragosa

Paul Newman

Sting

Rudy Giuliani

# # #

When I heard that one of my favorite comedians had been booked for the show, I came in early to hang out with him in our Green Room—the area where guests relax before appearing on a TV show. With his family-friendly sense of humor, I felt he had been a positive force in the entertainment industry for decades, and I wanted to express my admiration.

He came on our show to promote the Playboy Jazz Festival. He was joined by a group of talented teenaged musicians who were going to appear alongside him at the Hollywood Bowl. In fact, kids were everywhere, since about fifteen Little Leaguers were enjoying a behind-the-scenes tour with one of our videotape editors.

As he posed for photos with some of us before the show, the funny man more than lived up to my expectations. Marlon Brando once said, "Most of the successful people in Hollywood are failures as human beings." This guy seemed to be the exception. Though many celebrities are different people when the red light is turned off, he seemed to be the real deal.

After he appeared on our show, he agreed to pose for more photos on a stage ramp outside. He even beckoned an attractive female producer who earlier missed her chance for a picture because he was needed on set. I watched her excitedly hurry up the ramp to stand next to this icon amidst the boisterous kids.

Just before the camera clicked, the woman let out a shriek. The comedian had a smirk on his face like he had just told a dirty joke. At first, I thought they were simply being exuberant amidst the excited children. The truth was not so pretty.

Several of us watched in horror as the woman struggled to get away from the comedian. Moments later, she managed to make it to the edge of the ramp. As she jumped several feet to the ground, he slapped her behind.

"That creep groped me!" she exclaimed moments after she reached the ground. Although clearly shaken, she had enough presence of mind to say it out of earshot of the kids. "He not only grabbed me once but *twice!*"

Those of us who witnessed it all were speechless. I can only hope the children were oblivious to the repulsive drama. This wasn't some immature rock star trying to stupidly show his manhood. This was one of the most popular men in America, whose clean image transcended race, age, and gender... *Bill Cosby.*

Bill Cosby, minutes before the assault

We watched in stunned silence as he took off in his limousine as if nothing had happened. I told my coworker I'd back her up if she ever wanted to report it but, as far as

I know, she never did. Sadly, she was up against the same horrible quandary that countless other female assault victims face: Will they believe me? Do I want to relive this over and over again? Is it worth reporting, since nothing may come of it?

A few years later, many other women faced the same dilemma when they accused this supposed paragon of decency and family values of even more vile acts. Given what I witnessed, I don't doubt the possibilities.

CHAPTER 30
CAN'T STOP THE MUSIC

ON THE KTLA MORNING NEWS, we prided ourselves on doing it up right for each holiday. On Halloween, our anchors were known to dress up in full-costume regalia. On Thanksgiving, culinary experts manned a "Turkey Hotline," so viewers could call in for cooking tips. And as Valentine's Day approached, we aired live, surprise marriage proposals.

Independence Day was no exception to the holiday fun at KTLA. For the 4th of July in 2003, the obvious theme was patriotism. The highlight of the broadcast was to be presented at the end of show with a performance of "The Stars and Stripes Forever" by the United States Marine Band.

This was a big deal. Formed in 1798 by an Act of Congress, the United States Marine Band is known as "The President's Own" and is America's oldest continuously active professional musical organization. It was quite a coup for us to book them on the show, especially on our nation's birthday.

The United States Marine Band (Courtesy: U.S. Navy)

My job that sunny Friday morning was to make sure the performance went off without a hitch. I felt a sense of pride as I mingled before the show with these highly disciplined men and women attired in their scarlet dress coats, striped trousers, white tassels, and gold Marine Corps emblems. I even found myself standing a little taller and sucking in my gut. Our anchorwoman, Giselle Fernandez, had a somewhat different reaction.

"Hi, cutie," she said to the band's steely-eyed conductor when I introduced her to him. "I've always loved a man in uniform."

After ignoring Giselle's coquetry, the Marine Band's conductor joined me in the Green Room to watch the show. It wasn't large enough to hold all the musicians, so most of them wandered around the parking lot just outside the studio. Since it was about seven o'clock in the morning and they weren't on until just before nine o'clock, the conductor and I spent a long time sitting across from each other.

It felt even longer thanks to our lack of conversation.

Every time I brought up a topic, he'd just nod his head or mumble a two- or three-word answer—except when it came to the United States Marine Band. He proudly told me that John Philip Sousa himself, the man who composed "The Stars and Stripes Forever," led the band for twelve years, and he was honored to follow in his example. He mentioned his ensemble had traveled a long way to be on our show and he looked forward to their performance.

As the show entered its final half hour, it was obvious things were running behind schedule. Breaking news stories had eaten up airtime—something no one could foresee. About half past eight, I checked with the control room and learned we might not have time for the band's entire performance. Since it was scheduled for the end of the show, they could start the song and play as long as possible, even through the rolling credits.

I nervously walked back into the Green Room, trying to figure out how I was going to break the news to the conductor. It seemed unpatriotic to have to tell him the "Stars and Stripes" could not actually go on forever. In fact, it may have to be cut in half.

I waited a few minutes, hoping the show would make up for lost time. No such luck. As the band set up on the stage during the show's final commercial break, I inhaled a deep breath then proceeded to share the bad news with the conductor.

"That is totally unacceptable! We always play that song in its entirety!"

You haven't lived until you've had a United States Marine bark at you, nose-to-nose. I felt like a boot camp recruit facing his enraged drill sergeant.

I decided to take an optimistic approach. "Well, let's just proceed as planned. There just may be time to air the entire song. You never know what will happen in showbiz." I informed the show's director of the dilemma and hoped for the best. The conductor tended to his band while I stood off camera to watch the pending drama unfold. The math didn't add up. With our introduction, the segment with the song would run about four minutes. But, after the commercial, there would be less than three minutes left in the show. The only way the full song would be heard is if upper management decided to let the show run long, which meant cancelling some commercials. In the past, that had only occurred if there was a major breaking-news story.

"You're going to air the entire song, right?" the conductor said to me seconds before the segment began.

"*Uh*, sure," I mumbled while trying to avoid eye contact with him. I still held out hope we could somehow pull it off.

I quietly told anchorman Carlos Amezcua to keep his introduction brief to save time for the performance. When we came out of the commercial break, Carlos lived up to his reputation as a consummate professional.

"On our nation's birthday, it is an honor to end our show with the one and only United States Marine Band performing 'The Stars and Stripes Forever'!"

With crashing cymbals, blaring brass, and chirping piccolos, the rousing anthem shook the studio. Even the most jaded stagehands were overcome by patriotic fever. I found myself marching in step to the familiar tune. That is until I noticed an alarming sight on the studio monitor—the credits were starting to roll.

That meant we were going off the air in a matter of seconds, and the song was barely half over. The conductor had no clue that his beloved band was about to be cut off.

Perhaps this is a good time for me to slip out of the studio and let someone else endure the wrath of the United States Marine

Corps.

But I didn't shirk my duties. I stood by and watched the monitor go blank just as the horn section hit a crescendo. Floor director Neil Levine shouted the same words he said at the end of every show, "We're clear. Great job, everybody!"

The conductor looked like he was ready to lead his troops into battle. To be honest, I understood his anger. As far as I knew, this was the first time in history that the song designated by the United States Congress as our official National March had been rudely interrupted.

I did my best to calm the situation. "Sir, there's no way I could have predicted there would be so much breaking news. Next time, we'll put you on earlier in the show."

The conductor stomped off, but a tuba player spoke for him. "Don't worry. There won't be a next time."

I felt like a real schmuck. I was frustrated with management for not letting the show run long and angry with myself for not fighting harder to make it happen.

On a normal day, that would have been it. I would've returned to the newsroom to prepare for the next day's program. I'd learn from the experience and move on. But this being the 4th of July, KTLA had decided to throw a festive BBQ party in the parking lot for the entire station staff as well as the guests of that morning's show. Since dozens attended, I figured I could grab a quick bite and head back to the newsroom without being noticed.

No such luck.

Just as I was about to leave, I tossed what I thought was an empty plastic bag of BBQ sauce into a trashcan. It hit the side of the container and sprayed sticky, dark-brown liquid onto the pristine uniform of a female member of the Marine Band.

"I'm so sorry," I said. "If you send us your dry cleaning bill, we'll take care of it."

She didn't respond, but her expression told me I should never have gone to work that day.

When I got home later that afternoon, I asked Carole if she had seen the show.

"No, I decided to sleep in," she replied. "Were there fireworks?"

"Oh, you have no idea."

# # #

A month after the Marine Corps drama, Giselle resigned her co-anchor position to make documentaries. After a series of on-air auditions, she was replaced by Michaela Pereira. Both she and Carlos Amezcua are not only two of the most talented anchors on TV, but were a pleasure to work with as well.

Covering the Salt Lake City Winter Olympics with Carlos Amezcua

But the changes at work were nothing compared to my personal life.

After careful consideration, I decided Carole was "the one."

I wanted to surprise her with something special, so I invited her to meet me at the Hotel Bel Air. She thought we were there just for dinner, but I had loftier plans. When the waiter arrived with dessert, he presented her with a dome-covered silver platter. After he dramatically lifted the cover, he unveiled a velvet box that held a shiny little item I'd given to the maître d' earlier in the day: a sparkling diamond engagement ring.

I popped the question, and, lucky for me, Carole said, "Yes."

# # #

My engagement to Carole diminished the power of my mistress somewhat, but not enough for me to leave broadcasting altogether. Instead, we stepped into an "arrangement" where Carole and I tolerated her enough to benefit from the paychecks and perks.

In addition to introducing me to leaders in all walks of life, my mistress was also good to my kids. After I produced a segment on billionaire basketball team owners Joe and Gavin Maloof, they invited my son Philip to be a ball boy when their Sacramento Kings played the L.A. Lakers in the 2002 NBA Western Conference playoffs. My mistress also made it possible for my son Chris to join me at Shaquille O'Neal's mansion, where we hung out with Shaq and shot baskets on his home court.

Then there was the time my mistress arranged a meeting between me and the future leader of the free world.

CHAPTER 31
HAIL TO THE CHIEF

IN THE SUMMER of 2004, as Carole and I were planning our fall wedding, a skinny guy with a funny name seemed to come out of nowhere.

Barack Obama wasn't even a U.S. senator yet, but he gave a speech at the Democratic National Convention that ignited a political firestorm. His seventeen-minute keynote address was so powerful, he was interrupted thirty-three times by applause. Many political analysts wondered if he outshined the party's nominee, John Kerry.

When we got word that Obama was going to make a brief stopover in L.A., Michaela Pereira was determined to get an interview with him. But Obama was only available early in the morning and only at his airport hotel. Michaela had to be in the studio to co-anchor the show, so Executive Producer Rich Goldner came up with a backup plan.

"Ken, we need you to meet Obama near LAX tomorrow morning and field-produce a live satellite interview with Michaela," Rich said. "Got him slotted right after the top of the show at 7:05."

I looked forward to meeting the rising political star, even if it meant losing my beauty sleep in order to be at the airport in plenty of time. "Just tell me when and where."

"He's staying at the LAX Sheraton on Century Boulevard. He'll meet you in the lobby. We rented a conference room down the hall for the interview. It'll have to be quick, since he's got an 8:30 plane to catch."

Later in the day, I called my parents in Newport Beach and happened to mention who I was meeting in the morning.

"I'm excited to hear what he's like in person," my mom said. She and my dad were lifelong Democrats in a sea of Republicans. She once told me being a liberal in ultra-conservative Newport Beach is like being a vegetarian in a steak house. People tolerate you but look at you with suspicion.

That night, I plotted my plan. Go to bed early, wake at five, hit the road about a half hour later, then be at the hotel in plenty of time to meet Obama and set up the shot with the camera crew.

The next morning started smoothly. Soon I was cruisin' down the Harbor Freeway, blasting the radio. In 2004, it was hard to beat the group OutKast to get your heart pumping in the morning:

"I like the waaaay you move. I like the waaaay you move."

Before I left home, Mapquest advised me it would take forty-six minutes to get from South Pasadena to the LAX Sheraton. Of course, it had no way of knowing that, a mile ahead of me, a motorcyclist would go one-on-one with a semi-truck and lose. The freeway came to a complete halt. I switched to all-news radio, KNX, to find out what was going on.

"Look out for a SigAlert on the southbound Harbor Freeway at Exposition Boulevard by USC, where a motorcycle tangled up with a semi. Traffic is at standstill and may be for quite some time."

In an instant, I went from rockin' to the radio to swearing at my steering wheel. Ahead of me, it looked like the world's biggest used-car lot. I'd built in some padding time but didn't expect this.

My dashboard clock read 6:05. I tried to convince myself that, if nothing else went wrong, I could still make it in time. I just needed a good alternate route. Every veteran of the freeway capital of the world knows a few imaginative ways to navigate the concrete jungle.

I had two choices: take surface streets all the way to LAX or turn around and head up to the Santa Monica Freeway. Either way, I had to get out of the traffic jam fast.

Didn't the old Jetsons cartoons promise we'd have flying cars by now?

Traffic finally inched forward, and, thanks to a creative maneuver down the emergency lane, I made my way up to the alternate freeway. To my amazement, traffic was wide open, not a brake light in sight. The woman next to me in a Mercedes was trying to apply her makeup at sixty miles an hour.

I soon reached the San Diego Freeway, also known as the "405." Some say they call it that because traffic often moves at four or five miles an hour. Averaging 375,000 cars a day, it's the busiest freeway in the United States. But, for some reason, traffic was extremely light. It looked like half the city had slept in. I started to wonder if there was a special holiday nobody had told me about.

I more than made up for lost time; my good mood returned. I had only three miles to the Century Boulevard exit then a straight shot to the Sheraton. I figured my worries were over.

The voice on the radio told me that I figured wrong.

"Believe it or not, folks, we now have a second rush hour

SigAlert. This one's on the southbound San Diego Freeway at Century. Sure hope you don't have to get to LAX."

Within seconds, traffic came to a complete stop again. There could be only one explanation: God is a Republican and doesn't want me to put Obama on TV.

It was now about 6:40 a.m. Obama was due on the air in twenty-five minutes, and I was being stalked by SigAlerts. To make matters worse, KTLA had promoted his live appearance on the previous night's news and throughout the morning. I should be greeting him by now. Instead, I was staring at the back end of a Toyota with a bumper sticker that read: *My child is an honor student.*

I pictured Obama in the hotel lobby, talking to his aides. "Those guys made me skip breakfast, and now they're standing me up. No more interviews with KTLA."

I knew the camera crew wouldn't greet him, since they were setting up in the conference room down the hall. I probably should have called the office, but I refused to admit defeat. I could even see the LAX Sheraton in the distance.

With a few arm motions and a thank you wave, I convinced the other drivers to let me traverse three lanes to exit the freeway. I hung a right then gunned it down to Century Boulevard towards the Sheraton Hotel.

A noisy jumbo jet in final approach flew right overhead. If passengers had happened to glance down, they would have seen me break several traffic laws.

"Hey, Charlie, did you see that car run that stop sign?"

"Sure did."

"Guess it's true what they say about crazy California drivers."

Just as I ran a stop sign, my cell phone rang.

Busted. It's the Assignment Desk. They obviously know I'm

running late.

"Don't cancel the interview. I'm moments away," I pleaded then clicked off my phone.

I made my final approach and saw the best sight of the day: the fifteen-story LAX Sheraton. I bypassed the taxis and pulled up in front of the entrance, where a young valet casually chatted on the phone. No time for niceties. I tossed the kid my keys, told him I'd get my ticket later.

I bolted for the hotel door then stopped. No matter how late I was, I could afford five seconds to take a deep breath and calm down. After collecting myself, I strolled into the modern, spacious lobby.

A sharply dressed man in a suit and tie stood alone next to a potted palm. Six foot one and track-star thin, I spotted him at once.

"Mr. Obama?"

"Hi. Are you from KTLA?"

"Yes, I'm Ken Davis. Sorry for cutting it so close. Traffic was a nightmare."

His wide smile and firm handshake erased my guilt. "No problem. My flight plans changed," Obama said. "There's a nasty snow storm in Chicago, and my plane's delayed. I'll be lucky to get out this afternoon."

Relieved, I tried to relax. I hadn't angered the star of the show, and he wasn't in a big hurry, but the live interview started in five minutes.

Where the hell is the conference room?

Right on cue, a familiar face came to the rescue. I looked up to see a KTLA sound technician wave his hands at me from a nearby hallway.

"Mr. Obama, we're on the air in moments. Perhaps we should go," I said in the understatement of my career.

"Sure. And please call me Barack."

Barack Obama

My new buddy Barack and I briskly walked across the lobby toward the conference room. He got right down to business.

"So, this is a satellite interview with your anchorwoman. How does she pronounce her name?"

"Mi-kay-la. She's a big fan of yours."

"Good to hear. And what are we talking about?"

"Standard stuff. What it was like speaking at the convention, your political future, things you've been asked a hundred times before."

Actually, I had no idea what Michaela was going to ask, but the number-one job of a news producer is to keep the interview subject relaxed.

We headed down a short hallway and into the large

conference room. The camera crew had rearranged the furniture, set up the lighting, and placed a high-back chair about four feet in front of the camera.

The soundman showed Obama where to sit, gave him an earpiece, and applied powder to his forehead to hide any shine. I sat next to the cameraman, who was in no mood for pleasantries.

"It's about damn time," he whispered without looking up from his viewfinder.

A small monitor showed KTLA was in a commercial break leading up to our segment.

"Thirty seconds to air."

"Stand by."

"Here we go."

Michaela's face appeared on the monitor.

"This morning, we're pleased to talk with the man who shook the political landscape with his inspiring speech at this year's Democratic National Convention. *The Boston Globe* calls him, 'The future of the Democratic Party' and some are even saying he could become the first African-American president. He's U.S. senatorial candidate Barack Obama, and he joins us live from his Los Angeles hotel. Thanks for making time for us during your L.A. stopover."

"It's a pleasure to be here, Michaela," Obama said with a wide smile.

I can't recall the rest of the interview word-for-word, but I do remember Obama didn't want to talk about his presidential ambitions. At the time, he was a U.S. senatorial candidate from Illinois who had never held national office. His status would change the next month, when he won his election and was sworn in the following January as the fifth African-American United States senator in history.

When the five-minute interview ended, Obama grabbed

his Blackberry, and we strolled back into the lobby, where a young woman came up and asked for his autograph. I looked around to see if any other people recognized him, but, at this early stage of his career, he wasn't that well known outside of Illinois. After signing his name, Obama turned to me.

"I've got a few minutes. Are you hungry?"

Normally, I'd immediately return to the station after a field assignment. I decided not to be normal.

"You read my mind. I only had time for a little cereal this morning."

"You wanna grab a bite?"

"Let's do it."

Our choices were a crowded breakfast buffet or a half-empty espresso bar in the lobby. We chose the latter. Obama ordered iced tea and two protein bars. I went with a latte and a Danish. You never forget your first kiss or your first meal with a future president.

After we sat, I asked him a question that had bothered me since we met.

"So, why are you all by yourself?"

Obama chuckled. "I let my campaign aide fly home last night, so he could celebrate his wife's birthday today. He made it out just in time before the storm hit. I'm just fine on my own."

Trying to keep the conversation light, I asked about his days as a student in Southern California. "Didn't you go to Occidental College?"

"Sure did. I went to Oxy for a couple of years." He leaned back and managed a small smile. "Excellent school. That's where I gave my first political speech."

"What was it about?"

"We were protesting the school's investments in

apartheid South Africa. It was a lousy speech, and I only spoke for a minute or two at a rally. Felt like I was in a trance, speaking lines from a school play. Just when I got on a roll, it became time to leave the stage. Afterwards, I was convinced my public speaking days were over. Obviously, I later changed my mind."

He unleashed his now-famous wide-tooth grin then stretched out his lengthy arms across the top of the leather booth. Our discussion turned to politics.

"So, is 'The Governator' as popular as ever?" Obama asked with a gleam in his eye.

He was, of course, referring to Arnold Schwarzenegger, who had become California's governor in a recall election the year before.

"I guess so," I replied. "But I think he's a better actor than governor."

Now relaxed, a different Obama emerged, and it felt like I was breaking bread with an old college pal.

"Hey, you must know the Hollywood crowd. Ever meet Stevie Wonder?"

I sat a little taller in my seat. "Sure have. I met Stevie briefly, after he was on our morning news show. That guy sure glows with positive energy."

"I thank him for my marriage," Obama said. "If I wasn't a Stevie Wonder fan, I don't think Michelle would have gone out with me. We both like him so much that his song 'You and I' was our wedding dance."

After we covered show business, I'd love to say our conversation elevated to more weighty topics, like the crises in the Middle East or climate change. Instead, we discussed such important matters as... professional football.

"I can't understand why you guys don't have an NFL team here," Obama said.

"Makes no sense to me, either. At least we have the Lakers and Dodgers."

"And don't forget the USC Trojans," he added. I didn't bother to tell him I'm a bigger fan of USC's cross-town rivals, UCLA, since that's where my parents met.

Obama smiled then checked his Blackberry. I sensed our time together was about to end. Without thinking, I blurted out what was on my mind.

"I'm convinced you'll run for president someday."

He looked me right in the eyes. For a moment, I thought I was about to land a big scoop. Then reality set in. In an instant, I went from "Barack's buddy" to just another member of the media.

"Right now, all I'm concerned about is my senate race," he said, reverting back to political persona. He'd obviously dodged the subject many times before, but at least I gave it a shot.

After a quick comment about the beautiful Southern California weather, our breakfast break came to an end.

With a firm handshake, he gave me his best wishes then headed toward the elevator. As he walked away, a thought struck me. This guy had something special I'd seen in only three other public figures: Walter Cronkite, Ronald Reagan, and Bill Clinton. The instant you met them, you felt like you were their best friend, no matter what your politics. Call it charisma on steroids.

I went out to retrieve my car, apologizing to the valet for my abrupt arrival earlier in the morning. A fat tip expunged any hard feelings. I headed back to KTLA in Hollywood, unfazed by the heavy traffic. In fact, I welcomed the chance to reflect on my morning adventure. One more SigAlert and the morning would have been a total disaster. Instead, everything worked out just fine.

My only regret is that I didn't take a photo with him. In 2004, most cell phones didn't have cameras, and I felt uncomfortable asking politicians to pose for pictures; I'm supposed to be a journalist not a fan. But I must admit I'd love to have a snapshot of me hanging out with a future president to show my friends and family.

Even without a photo, this story is a common topic of conversation in our home when Obama's face appears on TV. To this day, Carole still likes to tell people the first thing I said when I came home that night.

"Honey, today I met a future president of the United States."

CHAPTER 32
BRAND NEW DAY

CAROLE AND I MARRIED on October 28, 2004, in Ocho Rios, Jamaica. The setting was perfect—a pristine, white-sand beach next to gorgeous turquoise waters. Soon after we returned home, we held a reception in the historic Chandelier Room at Santa Anita Racetrack and began plotting our escape from Hollywood.

Phil and Chris join us at our wedding reception (Photo by Victoria Arriola)

Carole was tired of living in the big city, and, after more than three decades, I was ready for a significant break from my mistress. The demands of the job had started to ramp up again. Also, I was in my early fifties and the writing was on the wall... I had become a "senior citizen" in the business.

Carole was more than happy to yank me away from my work. We both recognized the need for a fresh start. With our new marriage and both my sons doing well, it seemed the perfect time for us to get the heck outta Dodge.

The pieces came together when Carole was offered a position to help open a new Costco in San Luis Obispo. In addition, I received some money for helping in the development of a game show for ABC. The program never aired, but I still received a healthy check for my services.

We figured it was now or never, so we bought a small place up the California coast near Pismo Beach, and I quit KTLA. It's scary to walk away from a steady paycheck, but, once again, to quote Helen Keller, "Life is either a daring adventure, or it is nothing at all."

# # #

I love the ocean. Next to a beautiful woman, I think it's God's finest creation. Something about the sea casts a spell that stirs my heart and stimulates my imagination. It's the only place where salt lowers your blood pressure. Our little plot of land was a bit inland, but we could see and feel the alluring Pacific in the distance. If we listened closely, we could hear waves crashing at night. It was the perfect getaway for my weary brain. While Carole set to the task of helping to open a Costco, I set my sights on recharging my batteries.

Physical separation from the noise of broadcasting cleared my brain and allowed me to reflect on my relationship with my mistress. I cogitated on the times when I'd felt like the luckiest guy on Earth to walk hand in hand with this vexing siren. She introduced me to special people, showed me the world, and, together, we'd even played a part in the saving of lives. Thanks to her, it's a pretty good bet I was the only guy on the planet who could say he'd had breakfast with Barack, cocktails with Cronkite, and sang with Spector. Part of me was still in love with her and, I suppose, always would be.

But somewhere along the way, she lost her moral compass. By this point in my career, high quality, objective journalism had become a rare commodity.

I remembered Walter Cronkite telling me, "A reporter's only job is to hold up a clear mirror and truthfully show what happened. Opinions have no place in our business." Sadly, Uncle Walter's style of reporting seemed to be headed the way of the dinosaur and disco.

I had changed over the years, as well. I was tired of the insincerity, insecurity, and insanity of Tinsel Town. I'd seen too many of my colleagues abused and discarded. I needed something more tangible to hang on to.

After about six months of contemplation, reflective walks on the beach, and numerous late-morning sleep-ins, I reached a major decision: I needed to make a permanent break from my mistress.

But first, there was the matter of college tuition for both my sons and the funding of a decent retirement for Carole and me. A local radio station had offered me a job on a morning talk show, and I considered trying to teach a class at nearby Cal Poly University in San Luis Obispo.

But both these options paid peanuts compared to what I could earn in Hollywood. So I called on my mistress once again, for the sole purpose of beefing up my bank account.

CHAPTER 33
ONE LAST TIME

IN EARLY 2006, I heard that Cheri Brownlee, with whom I worked at *Real TV*, had started her own production company. I gave her a call, and it turned out she wanted me to begin on her latest show the following Monday.

Somehow, a daily 340-mile-roundtrip commute to work didn't seem like a wise idea, so Carole and I decided I'd rent a place in L.A. and take the train home every weekend. Amtrak's Pacific Surfliner offered a scenic, peaceful train ride that provided me a chance to unwind to and from the job and had a convenient stop near our place.

I figured I'd only work in Hollywood a few months. It turned out I wrote and produced almost non-stop for the next six years on nine different TV shows. Carole and I ended up moving back to Southern California.

Most of the programs I worked on only aired for a short time, but I got to indulge my love of storytelling and work with some of my favorite former colleagues, like producers Eddie Rohwedder, Gary Basmajian, and Jason Bourgault. The shows ran the gamut from *Shockwave* (History Channel), where we took viewers inside historical events with documentary-style reports; to *Disorderly Conduct* (Spike TV), where we featured cops capturing bad guys and hopefully taught some clueless clowns that it's not a good idea to drive drunk down the wrong way of the interstate with a baby in your lap; to *Untamed & Uncut* (Animal Planet), where we showed everything from parrots gone postal to horse rescues. Of all the shows I worked on in my career, this was my dog's favorite.

# # #

While working as the head writer for *Top Shot* (History Channel), I received devastating news. My father had been diagnosed with that cruel mind-robber, Alzheimer's disease. Since it was progressing rapidly, I felt I needed to take another break from the business to help both him and my mother. We tried experimental treatments, and everyone in the family did what we could to keep his deteriorating mind active. But we learned a hard truth: Alzheimer's is the only disease among the top-ten causes of death in America that cannot be prevented, cured, or even slowed.

Allen and Virginia Davis

Married 64 years

The last time I saw my dad was as he lay in his hospital bed in Newport Beach, California. In some ways, we were very different, but at that moment, we couldn't have been closer. It was as though we both knew it would be our final conversation.

"I'm proud to call you my father," I said with tears in my eyes.

He squeezed my hand. "You're a good son."

"I wasn't easy to raise, was I?"

He let out a hearty chuckle. "No, you weren't."

It felt good to hear him laugh again; it'd been so long. And yet it seemed he did it for me. The man who clowned around with sick kids at children's hospitals, played Santa during the holidays, and lifted the spirits of seniors when he delivered Meals on Wheels was intent on making me, his son, feel better.

I spoke the words that I didn't say enough during his lifetime: "I love you, Dad."

"I love you, too," he softly replied.

Then I instinctively did something I'd never done before—I leaned over and kissed him on his forehead.

It is said a young man will either try to emulate his father or will go the absolute opposite direction. In my early years, I saw my dad as "square" and undertook a mission to make my own unique, defiant way through the world. But, subconsciously, I must have admired him for his strong moral compass, kind heart, and selflessness, because those were the qualities I eventually tried to emulate in my adult years. As I looked at this gentle soul in his hospital bed, I realized how lucky I was to have him as my dad.

On June 22, 2010, my father peacefully passed away at the age of eighty-seven.

He was the kindest and most honorable man I've ever known.

# # #

When I returned to work, the time was perfect for trying something new and upbeat to snap me out of my somber mood.

The category is: Career Moves.

The question is: What can Ken Davis do that's fun, light, and positive?

And the answer is: Game shows!

The first was *It's Worth What?* (NBC), where contestants tried to guess the value of near-priceless treasures, such as a lock of JFK's hair or a dress worn by Princess Diana. I had a blast writing material for our comedian host, Cedric the Entertainer, but, sadly, *It's Worth What?* wasn't worth much in the ratings and only lasted nine episodes.

Since I'd enjoyed working on the previous game show, I thought I'd go for the bonus round and try it again with

You Deserve It (ABC). This program had two things going for it: we aired right after the hit show, *Dancing with the Stars;* and our host, Chris Harrison, was the popular star of *The Bachelor* and all its spinoffs. Alas, the ratings gods didn't find the show as deserving as I did and dumped us after the first season.

Next, my career took a supernatural turn when I produced segments for *My Ghost Story* (Biography Channel). Most of our guests were nice folks who truly believed they had encountered ghosts; others were as creepy as their stories. This was the only show I worked on where the guests had access to free alcoholic beverages, in case they got stage fright and required some liquid encouragement. Often, I was the one in need of a drink after hearing their spooky tales.

After I'd been with *My Ghost Story* for a few months, Carole's mother, Mimi, suffered several minor strokes. A strong-willed Costa Rican, she lived by herself for decades after losing her husband. But now, it was obvious she could no longer be alone.

The time had come to grapple with some critical choices that many adult children face regarding their aging parents: Do we hire a caregiver? Should we look into assisted living facilities? Would it be best if she moved in with us?

Carole's siblings showed little interest in helping with their mother's care giving. Carole, on the other hand, spent countless nights at her mother's side and was not about to let strangers take care of the woman who had lovingly raised her. The time had come to make a life-changing decision.

FAREWELL

To thine own self be true.

—William Shakespeare

CHAPTER 34
ROLLING IN THE DEEP

Fall 2012

BARACK OBAMA IS *re-elected to his second term as U.S. president; Adele lights up the music charts with "Set Fire to the Rain"; and I'm ready to finally call it quits with my mistress.*

# # #

I resigned from my position at *My Ghost Story* to become Mimi's caregiver. Recalling the importance of the loving care my dad received in his final years, it was a decision I instinctively knew I would never regret. At this point, Carole's career was much more stable than mine, so the selection of who would play this important role seemed obvious.

When Mimi and I weren't watching *Judge Judy* or humming along to *Lawrence Welk* reruns, I tried to get her out for a walk and fresh air but, except for a rare trip to the beach, she insisted on spending most of her time in bed.

Mimi enjoys a trip to Malibu

Our conversations were usually limited to mundane topics, like the weather or the dinner menu, until, one day, an old Mae West movie came on TV. Mimi's eyes lit up when I told her about the day I came across the screen legend's body.

"You should've yanked on her hair to see if she was wearing a blonde wig!" she said with a mischievous smile.

"Mimi, are you nuts?" I joked. "I had a serious case of the heebie-jeebies and just wanted to get the heck outta there."

Naturally, this led to me telling her about my other adventures with everyone from Phil Spector (whom she hated) to Walter Cronkite (whom she loved).

One day, after I'd told Mimi about Washoe the chimp, disco dancing in Acapulco, and other fond memories of my career, she got a wistful look in her eye.

"Do you miss it?"

I didn't want to lie to her and yet found myself saying, "Of course not, Mimi. You know I'd much rather be here with you."

After spending my entire adult life in broadcasting, much of my identity was, and probably always will be, intertwined with my career. Even though I'd recently hit sixty—in my line of work, roughly the same age as Moses—I continued to receive job offers that fed my self-esteem. But I knew, as I was aging, the business was in critical condition with no signs of recovery. As TV producer and former anchorwoman Kim Devore, with whom I worked at KNXT, told me, "Ken, when we began in our industry, it was about quality and ethics. Now, it's one continuous Junior Miss Pageant."

Bear with me as I pause for a brief editorial, but never in my lifetime have I seen such a full-blown assault on the truth by so-called journalists. I may sound like a nostalgic geezer longing for the good ol' days, but there's a reason why America's trust in the news media is at an all-time low. For someone who began in the business idolizing Walter Cronkite, "the most trusted man in America," that's hard to take.

If I had my way, television would be more PBS and less BS. Newscasts would air without commercials, so ratings would take a back seat and the focus would be on objective journalism instead of pimping glorified headlines for product promotions. Thirty-second political ads would be prohibited in favor of insightful debates, and advertising of any form would be banned from programs designed for children. Though I suspect I won't see any of these positive changes in my lifetime, I can still dream.

Too many people get their news only from biased media outlets and social connections that affirm their beliefs. Not only does this open the door to ignorance but also to fear of those who think differently. Some politicians and so-called journalists are more than happy to exploit this propensity for their own personal gain, to the detriment of a free and healthy society.

I'm convinced the most potent idea that civilization has ever produced is the belief that people can govern themselves. To sustain that, there must be a fair and non-partisan flow of accurate information. That's the role of the journalist. If a reporter can't be trusted to do their job, we are in dangerous times. Democracy and honest journalism rise and fall together.

History is littered with politicians discrediting the press in order to maintain control of the masses. When a credible news media isn't there to act as a spotlight and disinfectant, we give away our power as a people. That's why our forefathers put freedom of the press in the First Amendment.

To add to the problem, in the information age, anyone with a cellphone camera can call themselves a journalist. In the wise words of songwriter Tom Waits, "We are buried beneath the weight of information, which is being confused with knowledge."

One afternoon, while listening to the radio, I became incensed when I heard some pompous blowhard proclaim, "Ignore what the other so-called journalists report. Only I will give you the truth!" No matter if he was a liberal, conservative, or recent immigrant from Pluto, his words sickened me. This carnival barker was trying to convince his audience that the mainstream media had an evil agenda and—oh, by the way—only *he* could be trusted above all others.

I know from personal experience that the vast majority of my fellow journalists are ethical and trustworthy. They proudly put accuracy and fairness first. Sure, there are cable "news" programs that disguise their political agenda, but I never worked for them. In my experience, personal political opinions were rarely discussed in the newsroom. In fact, when I was at CBS News, we were strongly discouraged from even putting political bumper stickers on our cars, lest anyone think we had a personal agenda to promote.

One evening, I was talking with our good friends Greg and Cindy Gleich about the fact that any joker can call themself a journalist, even if they never graduated fifth grade. Why, I argued, don't we have an accredited program to separate so-called journalists from those who are trained and have pledged to uphold the highest standards of the profession? Lawyers must pass a bar exam, and top weather reporters are certified by the American Meteorology Association, so why not journalists? Maybe then the public would be more apt to trust their reporting.

To become one of journalism's elites, one would have to complete a meticulous academic program led by acclaimed professionals where they publicly commit to uphold a strict code of ethics. In addition to the ones I mentioned earlier that we followed at PBS, the list could include some of these already outlined by the Society of Professional Journalists:

> ➤ Take responsibility for the accuracy of your work. Verify information before releasing it. Use original sources whenever possible.
> ➤ Avoid stereotyping. Journalists must examine the ways their values and experiences may shape their reporting.
> ➤ Diligently seek interviewees who have been the subject of negative news coverage; allow them to respond to criticism or allegations of wrongdoing.
> ➤ Support the open and civil exchange of views, even views you find repugnant.

And one that I heard on my first day of Journalism class back at Northern Arizona University:

> ➤ Give voice to the voiceless.

When Cindy and Greg agreed that I might be on to something, my confidence kicked into high gear, so I continued with my speculations.

After successfully completing the program and, more importantly, while continuing to uphold the code of ethics, these journalists could then be distinguished as "journologists" or some other fancy title. Whatever the designation, those with the distinction would gain credibility and become the pride of the profession.

Throughout the rest of the day, I became more and more convinced I had come up with a perfect plan to restore the public's confidence in the battered world of journalism.

That night, I drifted off to sleep thinking, *Man, am I brilliant.*

The next morning, I awoke thinking, *Man, am I ignorant.*

Who would get to decide which wannabees were worthy enough to gain the so-called "Seal of Approval"?

Wouldn't journalists without the accreditation complain it would stifle freedom of the press?

Would those who hate the press call it a cheap ploy of the corrupt media to further deceive the public?

Despite my trepidations, I decided to run my idea by the esteemed Joe Saltzman, a longtime veteran of the news business and a beloved professor at the USC Annenberg School for Communication and Journalism.

"Your plan is as valid as any I've ever heard, Ken. You've hit on a dilemma that has plagued journalists since the beginning of time." But the good professor wasn't quite ready to give me an A-plus. In addition to the concerns I'd already considered about my own proposal, he came up with a few more. To paraphrase his thoughts:

Beyond the journalists "without accreditation" taking issue with it, many in academia would also consider the idea fraught with peril for the future of free and unfettered journalism.

What about journalists who didn't want to or couldn't afford to participate in such a program? Would they be ostracized?

And, worst case scenario, it could create a "hate" list that a corrupt government could use to harass, imprison, or even murder journalists—something that has happened repeatedly in other countries around the world.

Joe also correctly pointed out that few people under thirty rely on traditional news media anymore. Most get their news from the Internet, from social media, from friends and clergy. What happens to journalism if today's established media eventually go out of business? All time and effort into the concept could be wasted.

So, I asked Joe what he would do to restore confidence in the news media.

"It might be enough if journalists would stop spouting their opinions on talk shows and just do their jobs," Joe replied. "Also, I don't have any understanding of what 'truth' or 'objectivity' are. These words are loaded with controversy and subjective feelings. What truth? Whose truth? And, since everyone has biases, prejudices, and feelings about everything, what in God's name is objectivity?"

"So, I tell my students all the time to forget about truth and objectivity. Be concerned about three things only:

Accuracy, Fairness, and Transparency. If a journalist strives for these more tangible pursuits, then all will be well."

Hard to argue with Joe, although I would add two more items to his suggestions for journalists:

- ✓ Remember, the story isn't about you.

- ✓ And...anyone with the last name of Kardashian is NOT news. Ever.

CHAPTER 35
MIDGETS ARE BIG THIS YEAR

DESPITE MY FRUSTRATION with the business, the beckoning call of my incessant former lover still made my heart race. Whether I liked it or not, in many ways I was just another broadcasting junkie looking for my next hit.

So, in a moment of temporary insanity, I came up with a lame-brained scheme where I could somehow stay home with Mimi while keeping my hand in the business. If I couldn't populate newsrooms with "journologists," at least I could try to improve the existing TV landscape with better programs.

One day, while Mimi slept, I snuck upstairs and called the latest personification of my mistress.

"Hi, Jessica. This is Ken Davis."

"Hey, Ken. Long time no talk. How the heck are ya?"

Jessica Miller and I worked together on a TV show several years earlier where I was a senior producer and she was relatively new to the business. After that, her career went into fast-forward and now—at the "seasoned" age of twenty-eight—she was head of development for a television production company. In a business that worships youth, it's not unusual to see someone under thirty in a position of major power.

"Jessica, I've got some show proposals I want to run by you. You got any free time coming up?"

"Sure. How 'bout lunch on Wednesday?"

We decided to meet at a chic Malibu eatery. My plan was to present eight concepts for quality TV shows, with the hope that her company would be interested in producing at least one of them. In addition to paying me for the ideas, they could hire me as a consultant working from home. Not only could I continue as Mimi's caretaker, I could also successfully maintain a long-distance relationship with my mistress.

On the day of the lunch, Carole arranged for someone else to watch her mom. I jumped in my car, excited about my upcoming meeting. I knew my ideas not only had the requisite bells and whistles necessary for successful TV shows, but most of them had redeeming social value—something quickly disappearing from the vast television landscape.

My eight proposals included: A show where talented but struggling musicians from impoverished countries are flown to the U.S. to share the stage with their favorite superstars; a program where the leaders of the major political parties debate a different hot topic each week as they are questioned by sharp-witted college students; and a game show where people from different cultural and economic backgrounds work together to see who can best help needy families.

It's estimated that less than one-percent of network show ideas ever make it to air, but, as I strutted into the restaurant, I felt sure Jessica would get fired-up by some of my proposals.

After pleasantries, we got down to business.

Normally, in a meeting like this, I would give a spirited

presentation about each show and then deliver to the person who holds my future in her hands a short, typed proposal to take home for thoughtful consideration. But, since we were out in public, Jessica insisted on quietly reading my ideas to herself. "To keep them away from prying ears," she insisted.

I wasn't pleased, since I had memorized a compelling sales pitch for each show. All I could do was sit back and watch as she looked through my proposals. Nothing like having the last breath of your resuscitated career in the hands of someone who's young enough to be your daughter.

When she glanced at the first proposal, she revealed a little smile.

She likes it! Man, I'm a friggin' genius.

After about ten seconds, she looked up at me and uttered perhaps the most decisive word in the English language… a word that leaves no doubt about how the speaker really feels… a word that makes or breaks relationships in an instant:

"No."

My other proposals elicited similar responses, such as: "Nope," "Nah," and "Not gonna work." When I went zero-for-eight, my defenses kicked in.

How dare she not like my ideas? What does this naïve neophyte know about the television business anyway?

I did my best to keep my cool, but Jessica sensed my frustration.

"Ken, I want to let you in on a secret. I was talking with my colleagues the other day, and we're convinced we know the next TV trend. If there's any way you could incorporate it into one of your show ideas, I think we can do business."

I leaned in closer to hear the magic formula. Whatever

it was, I knew I could make it work.

"Trust me," I whispered. "I promise to keep it a secret."

Jessica glanced around the restaurant then locked eyes with me.

"Midgets."

The restaurant became so quiet you could hear a mouse fart.

"Excuse me? It sounded like you said midgets."

"I did. Just hear me out. Our research shows viewers get a kick out of watching little folks. How about a comedy show starring midget bartenders? I hear they have them in Vegas and they're a riot. There's also midget wrestling and even dwarf tossing, but I don't think we could get away with showing that. The bottom line is… midgets are big this year."

Midgets are big this year?

I didn't know whether to laugh or cry. How could she say that with a straight face? I had nothing against doing a positive show about little people, but I sure wasn't going to have anything to do with making fun of them.

I wanted to respond, "I don't give a damn about your fancy job title. I've worked on more TV shows than you've had birthdays. It's because of people like you that television has become one continuous vaudeville show."

But I wimped out and responded, "*Uh*, let me think about it."

There wasn't a chance in hell I was going to consider it. In fact, the mere thought made me lose my appetite.

As for her, she remained unfazed by my lackluster response. Probably didn't matter to her one way or the other, since we both knew she'd have no problem finding someone willing to produce a show about almost anything, no matter how demeaning the subject manner.

A few minutes later, I bid farewell to the last personification of my mistress, the broadcasting business, and headed for my car.

If Casey Kasem were still here, I would've asked him to spin the old Phil Spector-produced hit, "You've Lost that Lovin' Feeling," because, at that moment, that summed up how I felt about the broadcasting business.

CHAPTER 36

50 WAYS TO LEAVE YOUR LOVER

AS I DROVE HOME via Pacific Coast Highway, gazing at the crystal-blue sea, the truth became loud and clear.

I can't do this anymore.

Many experts believe the best way to kick an addiction is to go cold turkey, and I innately knew that was the only way to end my four-decade affair with my mistress.

I reflected on the little boy in Altadena listening to his transistor radio who thought his life would be perfect if he jumped into the arms of his childhood crush. He got what he thought he wanted—excitement, adventure, success. But he had no idea what he *needed*.

Throughout this journey, my complex seductress didn't make my quest easy. On the outside, she could be exciting and beautiful, but, on the inside, she was often greedy and ruthless. As a result, that little boy grew into a man who learned to never fully trust her.

Still, I give her credit for teaching me invaluable lessons I'll remember the rest of my days. Perhaps most importantly, I learned it doesn't matter if you are a hotshot in Hollywood or a plumber in Peoria—everyone has a story hidden inside; everyone has wounds to heal; everyone is human. As a result, I learned not to judge others too quickly (unless, of course, they happened to be a serial killer or a fan of *The Jerry Springer Show*).

Too often my mistress abused her considerable power. In a nation rich with brilliant thinkers, teachers, artists, and dreamers, she has the ability to inspire us and make us better human beings. However, as the industry grew, she gradually turned to feeding us a steady diet of whatever appeals to the lowest common denominator.

Maybe I inherited my father's eternal optimism, but I'm not ready to give up on her yet. I'm still hopeful that someone more intelligent than I will find a way to help my mistress reach her full potential and become a more positive influence on society.

I couldn't berate her much, for I was far from perfect myself and succumbed over and over to her vampish spell.

I regret being on the road so much when my kids were young.

I wish I had stayed longer with quality networks like PBS, CBS, and NBC and spent less time chasing a paycheck.

I should have refused to go to Nicole Simpson's family church to disturb and offend worshippers.

And, oh yeah, I probably shouldn't have smoked that joint before I rode with the Arizona Highway Patrol.

I was blessed to end up with the most supportive wife on the planet. My mistress didn't know who she'd be up against when Carole came into my life. She helped me get my priorities straight and made me a better man.

The Emmys, Golden Mikes, and Genesis Awards were nice to receive, but no honor has meant more than the fact that I was able to maintain a close relationship with my sons—despite a broken marriage and an unstable mistress. Happily, Jette and I have remained friendly and always put parenthood first. Both Chris and Philip turned out to be intelligent, caring young men, and nothing makes me prouder than to be their dad.

I've also been fortunate to have the unconditional support of my parents and my sister. Material things come and go but, if you're lucky, family will always be there.

Was I ambitious in my career? You bet I was—you don't get far in my business without drive and determination. But, thankfully for me and everyone around me, I never unearthed an ambition for power. I never desired to sit at a big desk and wield a magic wand, making everyone beneath me jump at my whim.

When I began in the business, my only ambitions were to enjoy my career and die of exhaustion rather than boredom. But as I matured, I discovered that wasn't enough. Sure, I loved my mistress, but I knew that love was a one-way street. To be content, I needed some things far more important: a loving family, true friends, and self-respect gained from knowing there were times I at least tried to make the world a better place.

A Rolling Stones song says, "You can't always get what you want." But, in the end, I was one of the lucky ones—I got both what I wanted *and* what I needed, and I've even come to understand the difference.

Following your dream usually means paying a price. But, despite everything my seductive mistress put me through, I have had a life far beyond the wildest dreams of that little boy who listened to his transistor radio tucked underneath his pillow.

Would I do it all again?

In the words of Walter Cronkite, "You betcha."

THE END

ACKNOWLEDGMENTS

IN ADDITION TO Carole, Chris, and Philip to whom this book is dedicated, I want to thank my mother, Virginia Davis, for her constant encouragement and helpful suggestions.

My lifelong friend Darryl Meathe urged me to write this memoir and has been supportive from the beginning. He knows me better than anyone but has stood by me anyway.

Kathryn Galán enhanced all she touched through her first-class production skills and advice. I'm also grateful for the insightful story development ideas of Susan Maddy Jones and the astute editing talents of Brian Whyte. Marcia Smart, Gail Field, and Sheli Ellsworth were always willing to lend their creative brains to make this a better book.

I appreciate the moral support of Rick Kurshner, Stephanie Cutler Pflaster, Bill Knoke, Jayne Merritt, Don Barrett, Christina Steiner, Mark Gronwald, Len Lamensdorf, and Joe Menkin. I will forever be grateful to the finest physician on the planet, Dr. Gregory Giesler.

Finally, I want to acknowledge my sixth-grade teacher, who once told me, "Kenny, you could fill a book with what you don't know." Well, Mrs. Counts, here is that book.

ABOUT THE AUTHOR

KEN DAVIS is a three-time Emmy-award-winning writer, producer, and on-air reporter who has worked for all the major networks in news, entertainment, and reality TV. At the age of twenty, he became the nation's youngest TV anchorman and went on to work with Walter Cronkite, Dan Rather, and dozens of other prominent broadcasters and entertainers. He also hosted the PBS program *Why in the World?* and has reported stories for *The MacNeil/Lehrer NewsHour,* as well as breaking news reports for CBS and KTLA-TV. In addition to his Emmys, Davis has been honored with three Golden Mikes, two Genesis Awards, and is a member of the John Muir High School (Pasadena, CA) distinguished alumni Hall of Fame. He and his wife, Carole, make their home in Southern California.

CRCRCR

Made in the USA
Monee, IL
29 June 2020